exploring

PACKAGE DESIGN

Chuck Groth

THOMSON

DELMAR LEARNING ™   Australia Canada Mexico Singapore Spain United Kingdom United States

THOMSON

DELMAR LEARNING

Exploring Package Design
Chuck Groth

Vice President, Technology and Trades SBU:
David Garza

Director of Learning Solutions:
Sandy Clark

Senior Acquisitions Editor:
James Gish

Development Editor:
Jaimie Weiss

Channel Manager:
William Lawrensen

Marketing Coordinator:
Mark Pierro

Production Director:
Mary Ellen Black

Senior Production Manager:
Larry Main

Production Editor:
Benj Gleeksman

Editorial Assistant:
Niamh Matthews

Library of Congress Cataloging-in-Publication Data:
Groth, Chuck
    Exploring package design / Chuck Groth. p. cm.
    Includes bibliographical references and index.
ISBN 1-4018-7217-4
1. Packaging--Design. I. Title.
    TS195.4.G76 2006
    741.6--dc22   200503831

ISBN: 1-4018-9918-8

NOTICE TO THE READER

To Dijana —

patient wife, compassionate friend and the source of all my energies and inspirations.

And to my sons, Elliott and David, for being who you are: true and breathtaking, you are my reassurance and reason.

table of contents

TABLE OF CONTENTS

exploring package design

preface

INTENDED AUDIENCE

Package design is one of the more complex specializations in the field of graphic communications. Translating a design concept across three-dimensional surfaces requires planning, creativity and an understanding of market perception. *Exploring Package Design* is written for those students of graphic design—whether those working toward a degree or professionals looking to expand their knowledge and skills—who are eager and willing to undertake the challenge of applying a vision, including color palette, typographic voice, imagery, and structural exploration to the discipline of package design.

Among those for whom this book is intended:

- Students studying graphic design at the college level

- Vocational students whose talents and inclinations lean them toward three-dimensional design and package design

- Design professionals who are open to the opportunity of expanding their experience, skill sets, and market understanding

- Those interested in the history, psychology and techniques of packaging.

Exploring Package Design is written for instructors and designers at every level of their craft who are looking for a resource to aid them in the field of package design.

BACKGROUND OF THIS TEXT

I have been working in the field as a graphic designer for twenty five years, and I brought that experience to the classroom when I began my teaching career six years ago. Professional experience carries you pretty far in teaching, but there comes a time when a truly useful text can give additional cohesion to concepts for students. In the area of package design, however, I was not able to find a book that would serve students in a comprehensive way. By that, I mean there are books of 3-D patterns that teach structure but do not address communication; there are books that show photo after photo of beautifully designed packages, but tell the reader nothing of the engineering that went into the pieces or the production processes involved.

Over the years, I've put together a series of assignments for my students to explore all the concerns of the designer that chooses to go into the field of package design. This book grew from those assignments, those students that met the challenge and the need for a textbook that followed the process of package design from start to finish.

While this book sets out to demystify the process of package design, it does presuppose that the reader has a basic knowledge and understanding of some design fundamentals. A familiarity with board techniques is almost essential, as is a background in color theory, effective typographic design and a degree of creativity and presentation skills.

TEXTBOOK ORGANIZATION

This book has been organized to present the subject of package design both academically and practically. From the history of packaging to the description of forms and techniques for producing professional-quality package mock-ups, the process of packaging is explained in clear, easy to follow chapters.

Each chapter includes the following:

- An introduction to the specific topic

- An in-depth body of text covering the subject of the chapter

- Illustrations and diagrams

- A series of practical and conceptual exercises that reinforce the covered material

- Review questions on the chapter material for class or self-study

Chapter One describes the history of packaging, from the natural containers used by early civilizations to the modern materials, structures and design concerns of today.

Chapter Two introduces the tools commonly used by designers, as well as the basic forms of packaging. Learning to recognize design paradigms is emphasized, with examples.

Chapters Three through Six guide the reader through the process of producing 3-D mockups from flat patterns, including package construction and board techniques, understanding special processes and the study of 2-D templates to best choose an appropriate package form.

Chapter Seven explores the marketing of packages through point-of-purchase displays. Effective design and placement of P.O.P. displays is discussed along with modifiable patterns for several common displays.

Chapters Eight and Nine focus on applying the craft of package design to a career. Portfolio options are evaluated and techniques are described for photographing and presenting work. Professional affiliations and organizations are introduced for the package designer.

The book text is followed by several useful directories of graphic design and packaging organizations and affiliations, contributors and a list of further reading suggestions.

FEATURES

- An essential text for anyone interested in package design.

- Clear, organized and easy to understand, this book leads the reader through the process of package design, from identification of audience, conceptualization, development, to high-quality mock-ups.

- An excellent resource of the step-by-step of package design, useful package patterns and a brief history of the field.

- Concepts and principles are brought to life through case studies of projects by graphic designers and interviews and quotes by established package design professionals.

SPECIAL FEATURES

▶ Objectives

Learning objectives start off each chapter. They describe the competencies the reader should achieve upon understanding the chapter material.

▶ Tips and Quotes

Tips provide special hints, practical techniques, and information to the reader. Quotes from industry professionals also provide industry advice and inspiration.

▶ Sidebars

Sidebars appear throughout the text, offering additional valuable information on specific topics.

▶ Professional Profiles

These career profiles, located throughout the book, allow the reader to learn from the example of successful designers who have won recognition in the field. Samples from their portfolios are included.

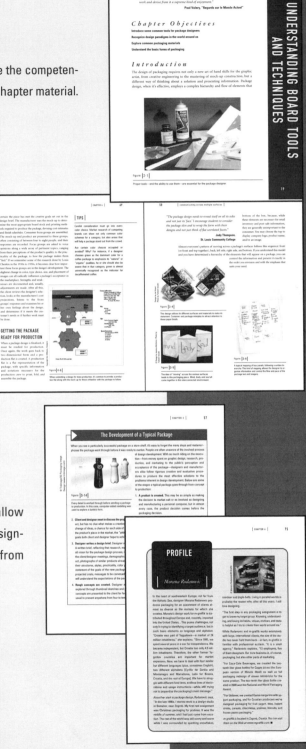

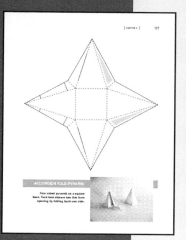

▶ Templates

Package templates provide easy-to-follow patterns for creating and assembling a variety of 3-dimensional packaging forms. A photograph of the assembled form accompanies each package template.

▶ Case Studies

Case studies follow several packaging projects from concept to completion, with step-by-step explanation of the process.

▶ Review Questions and Exercises

Review Questions and Exercises are located at the end of each chapter and allow readers to assess their understanding of the chapter. Exercises are intended to reinforce chapter material through practical application.

E.RESOURCE

This guide on CD was developed to assist instructors in planning and implementing their instructional programs. It includes sample syllabi for using this book in either an 11 or 15 week semester. It also provides chapter review questions and answers, exercises, PowerPoint slides highlighting the main topics, and additional instructor resources.

ISBN: 1-4018-7217-4

ABOUT THE AUTHOR

Chuck Groth has been a professional graphic artist since 1978, and has worked on staff as a designer and illustrator at the Kansas City Star, the Wichita Eagle and the St. Louis Post-Dispatch and as Director of Groth Graphic Design, a design and illustration studio. His clients include McDonnell-Douglas Aircraft, the Associated Press, Purina Mills, Adriatic Travel, Willow Music, Hallmark Cards, The American Heart Association and the Washington Post, among others. He has taught package design at Maryville University in St. Louis, Missouri and is currently an Assistant Professor of Graphic Communications at St. Louis Community College where he teaches graphic design, drawing for graphics, illustration and package design.

A graduate of the University of Kansas, Groth studied with some of the most prestigious artists in the graphics field such as Ann Willoughby (principal of Willoughby Design Group and Director on the National Board of the American Institute of Graphic Arts) and noted illustrators Thomas B. Allen and James McMullen.

In addition to teaching full time, Groth has served as a Graphic Communications advisory board member, faculty sponsor of a student AIGA chapter and graphic design club, and written college courses in package design. He has been nominated four times for inclusion in "Who's Who Among America's Teachers."

ACKNOWLEDGMENTS

I would like to give heartfelt thanks to Senior Acquisitions Editor Jim Gish, for encouragement and guidance, Development Editor Jamie Weiss, for keeping me on task, and everyone at Thomson Delmar Learning that helped bring this book from an idea to a reality.

Thanks, also, to my friends and colleagues at Meramec College, to my students, who taught me as well, and to everyone who smoothed my path and illuminated my way in the writing of this book.

Additionally, this book would not have been possible without the creative and compelling work contributed by packaging industry design professionals from around the world. At last count, over ten countries and dozens of states are represented in work and words.

—CG

Thomson Delmar Learning and the author would also like to thank the following reviewers for their valuable suggestions and expertise:

REID ANDERSON, Graphic Design Department, Durham College, Ontario, Canada

MICHAEL CIARCIA, Graphic Design Department, Westwood College, Atlanta, Georgia

CECE CUTSFORTH, Chairperson, Graphic Design Department, Portland Community College, Portland, Oregon

CHERIE FISTER, Art and Design Department, Maryville University, St. Louis, Missouri

ANDREA HESTOWSKI, Design Department, The University of Kansas, Lawrence, Kansas

TADASHI ISOZAKI, Design Department, The University of Kansas, Lawrence, Kansas

ROBERT MORRIS, Art Department, Penn Valley Community College, Kansas City, Missouri

NATHAN PIERATT, Graphic Design Department, Westwood College Online, Denver, Colorado

MICHAEL SPORZYNSKI, Communication Design Department, Parsons School of Design, New York, New York

PETE RIVARD, Graphics and Printing Technologies Department, Dunwoody College of Technology, Minneapolis, Minnesota

CONTRIBUTORS DESIGNERS / STUDIOS

A.M.
Associates(www.structuralpackaging.com)
Laurel Miller, Director
West Sussex, United Kingdom

Bader Design
Wendy Bader, Designer
St. Louis, Missouri

Bag Ladies Tea
(www.bagladiestea.com)
Boston, Mass

Behrman Communications (Burt's Bees)
(www.behrmancommunications.com)
New York, New York

Brewer-Riddiford
(www.brewer-riddiford.co.uk)
London, England

Boots
Brendan McElroy,
Creative Implementation Manager
Nottingham, United Kingdom

CHRW Advertising (zum)
(www.chrwadvertising.com)
Kansas City, Missouri

Dustin Commer

Crayon Design & Communication, Inc
(www.crayondesign.net)
Sol Lang, President
Montreal, Quebec, Canada

Giorgio Davanzo Design
(www.davanzodesign.com)
Giorgio Davanzo, Principal
Seattle, Washington

Cherie Fister, Associate Professor
Maryville University
St. Louis, Missouri

Graphical House
(www.graphicalhouse.com)
Glasgow, Scotland

Griffin Chase Oliver, Inc.
(www.griffinchaseoliver.com)
Reno, Nevada

Staci Hassan-Fowles Graphic Design /
Consulting
(www.portfolios.com/hassandesign)
Jamaica, West Indies

Henderson + Aurelio Design Associates, LLC
(www.hendersonaurelio.com)
Catherine Aurelio, Owner/Principal
Santa Cruz, California

Hornall Anderson Design Works
(www.hadw.com)
Seattle, Washington

Tadashi Isozaki, Assistant Professor
University of Kansas
Lawrence, Kansas

Jose Soto Desino
(www.portfolios.com/josesoto)
Jose Soto Grageda, Designer
Puebla, Mexico

CHAPTER 4

University of Kansas
(www.ku.edu)
Lawrence, Kansas
       Bradford Klemmer, Designer
       Jessica McEntire, Designer
       Jacob Day Steele, Designer
       Jai Hoyer, Designer

Carol King, Designer
(www.portfolios.com/CarolKing)
New York, New York

Liberty Richter
(www.libertyrichter.com)
Kathy Bonynge, Senior Product Manager
Saddle Brook, New Jersey

Elizabeth Linde, Designer
(www.coroflot.com/elinde)
Brooklyn, New York

Maryville University
(www.maryville.edu)

St. Louis, Missouri
       Jason Koebel, Designer
       Matt Bender, Designer

m-graffik
(www.m-graffik.com)
Morana Radanovic, Creative Director
Zagreb,Croatia

Randy Mosher Design
(www.randymosherdesign.com)
Randy Mosher, Principal
Chicago, Illinois

Obata Design
(www.obatadesign.com)
Claudia Moran, Vice President
St. Louis, Missouri

Paguirigan Branding and Design
(www.paguirigan.com)
Olympia, Washington

Dmitry Paperny Studio
(www.dmitrypaperny.com)
Dmitry Paperny, Principal
New York, New York

Pomegranate Design
(www.pomegranate-design.com)
Diane Benjamin, Principal
Brooklyn, New York

Product Visualization Services
Patrick Belford, Owner
(www.pvservices.com)
Toronto, Ontario, Canada

Public Image Design
(www.publicimagedesign.com)
Daryl Woods, Principal
Toronto, Canada

Sazas Design
(www.sazasdesign.com)
Helena Cabezas, Art Director
Manhattan, New York

St. Louis Community College at Meramec
(www.stlcc.edu)

St. Louis, Missouri
       April Kovarik, Designer
       Nicole Savory, Designer
       Daniel Shinn, Designer
       Dottie Detring, Designer
       Jessica Baechle, Designer
       Joseph Wisniewski, Designer

Studio GT&P / Pubblicita & Marketing
(www.tobanelli.it)

Gianluigi Tobanelli, Principal
Foligno, Italy

Tazo Tea
(www.tazo.com)
Andrea Drapcha, Creative Project Manager
Polara Studios, Inc, Photography
Seattle, Washington

Judith Thompson, Associate Professor
St. Louis Community College
St. Louis, Missouri

Tridimage 3D Packaging Image Design
(www.tridimage.com)
Hernan Braberman, Design Director
Ciudad de Buenos Aires, Argentina

VINE360
(www.vine360.com)
Joy Mac Donald, Creative Director
Edina, Minnesota

Mark Weisz Design
(www.markweisz.com)
Clifton, New Jersey

Hadiya Williams, Designer
(www.portfolios.com/hadiya)
Chicago, Illinois

Monghan (William) Wu, Designer
(www.portfolios.com/monghan)
Brooklyn, New York

CREATIVE SERVICES

The American Package Museum
(www.packagemuseum.com)
Ian House, Curator
Foster City, California

The Creative Group
(www.creativegroup.com)
Julie Sims, PR Manager
Menlo Park, California

The British Museum
(www.thebritishmuseum.ac.uk)
London, England

ICOGRADA (International Community of Graphic
Design Associations)
(www.icograda.org)
Brussels, Belgium

QUESTIONS AND FEEDBACK

Thomson Delmar Learning and the author welcome your questions and feedback. If you have suggestions that you think others would benefit from, please let us know and we will try to include them in the next edition.

To send us your questions and/or feedback, you can contact the publisher at:

Thomson Delmar Learning
Executive Woods
5 Maxwell Drive
Clifton Park, NY 12065
Attn: Media Arts & Design Team
800-998-7498

Or the author at:
Chuck Groth
St. Louis Community College at Meramec
11333 Big Bend Blvd
St. Louis, MO 63122

cgroth@stlcc.edu

CHAPTER

1

"Histories make men wise; poets, witty; the mathematics, subtle; philosophy, deep; logic and rhetoric, able to contend."

Francis Bacon (1561–1626)

Chapter Objectives

Define package design

Become familiar with the history of package design and the evolution of packaging materials

Understand the unique challenges of three-dimensional visual communication

Introduction

Throughout human history, we have had the need to devise containers. Any time surplus food, water, or other supplies and provisions existed, methods to store, protect, and transport them have been required. The very earliest examples were undoubtedly provided by nature: hollow gourds, containers fashioned from woven or

figure |1-1|

Some of the earliest containers were provided by Nature.

matted fibers and leaves, animal skins and bladders, even mud and clay all served as some of the ready-made containers employed by our hunter-gatherer ancestors. As technology and society became more complex, of course, so did our need for more reliable alternatives.

ROOTS

We can trace examples of pottery back more than 8,000 years, when the art of ceramics began in the Middle East. We know that 5,000 years ago, Egyptians were creating wooden boxes and barrels. Thirty-five hundred years ago, the invention of the potter's wheel allowed for mass production of ceramic pots and vessels. The Phoenicians are credited with developing the technique of glassblowing 3,000 years ago. As far back as 2,000 years ago, the invention of true paper is attributed to a Chinese governmental official named Ts'ai Lun, the process of which remained more or less unchanged for centuries.

From these first steps, the timeline gets tighter. The first recorded use of "paper grocer's bags" appeared in 1630. Seventeen hundred saw the construction of a large-scale commercial glass factory in the United Kingdom, which could produce 3 million bottles in a year. The process of hot-canning food was patented in 1810. A synthetic plastic—called "Parkesine"—was produced in England in 1862, followed by celluloid in the United States in 1863. And an American bag maker named Robert Gair developed the first factory-produced folding cardboard boxes in 1890. As far as efficient containers go, we've had our hand in the game for a while and become pretty good at it. But where can we say the business of containment began to evolve into the art of package design? At what point does "packing" become "packaging"? It's probably a good idea to first get our semantics in order. Packing—the verb—is generally defined as the task of putting things into containers, usually for storage or transport. Surely, all the styles of containers mentioned earlier are useful in packing. When an object needs to be stored, preserved, and transported, the proper packing is essential to prevent breakage or spoiling. The word "packaging," however, has another focus. Packaging—a noun—is the wrapping or container in which an item is presented for sale, or the design or style of the container in which something is offered for sale, especially from the point of view of its appeal. The first is concerned with practicality; the second must consider both function and aesthetic. It's been said that the eggshell is Nature's "perfect package." And as a natural container, the egg is almost unrivaled. Strong, lightweight, and protective of its contents, it represents Nature at its industrial best. But each egg is designed to look like every other egg—individuality has no part in the eggshell, nor is there specific information of what's inside or promise of superior contents. The eggshell is an ideal container, but not a package. So, we distinguish package design by its ability to convey information, to communicate.

Although the craft of creating utilitarian containers was widely practiced throughout the ancient world, the instances of true packaging were few. While certain items might have called for specifically shaped and sized containers, the concept of labeling was not common. There are numerous examples of jars and boxes dating to 3000–1000 B.C. found during the flurry of Egyptian excavations in the nineteenth century, and while many are painted or inscribed with the names of reigning pharaohs, dates, or commemorative notices, they don't speak to the contents within. Notable exceptions are the funereal canopic jars used in the preservation of Egyptian mummies and stored in the tomb near the celebrated body. Each jar held an important organ of the body, was labeled in hieroglyphics, and their lids were formed in the shape of that organ's protective god: The Falcon (Kebehsenuef) held the intestines; the Baboon (Hapi) contained the lungs; the Human

Courtesy of The British Museum

figure |1-2|

Canopic jars; 1070–712 B.C.; limestone. In ancient Egypt, canopic jars held internal organs of mummified dignitaries. Each jar was labeled and its lid fashioned in the shape of four heads—falcon, jackal, baboon, and human—which represented four protective gods.

(Imsety) held the liver, and the stomach was placed in the Jackal (Duamutef). In this case, information of the contents was very important and had to be unambiguous. Interestingly, in later periods of Egyptian mummification, the organs were preserved in linen and placed within the sarcophagus; embalmers began using fake canopic jars, which were solid. The religious aspects of the funeral rites were entirely overtaken by the aesthetic aspects.

Another important package of the ancient world was the clay Canaanite jar—also referred to as the amphora. Tall, slender, and strong, they were used widely in the area of the Mediterranean because they were easily stacked and transported by land or sea throughout the region. The Canaanite jar appeared as early as 1800 B.C. and went virtually unchanged for more than two thousand years. Some have been found inscribed with detailed information of their contents, which described not only the product within, but where it was made, by whom, and how it was to be used.

Courtesy of The British Museum, London

figure |1-3|

Canaanite jar; clay pot; Rome, Italy; 625 B.C. The Canaanite jar became one of the most recognizable containers of the ancient Mediterranean region.

| SURVEY |

Do you think that today's designers really need to know or learn about the history of design?

It is important to know/learn about design history.

I strongly agree.	**84%**
I agree.	**17%**
I disagree.	**2%**

Totals shown may be more or less than 100% due to rounding.

SOURCE: The International Council of Graphic Design Associations

figure |1-4|

Napoleon Bonaparte knew that an army moves on its stomach.

Glassmaking continued fairly uninterruptedly from its first rudimentary techniques—pressing heated glass into molds or around solid cores that were later dug out when the glass cooled—on through the invention of the glassblowing pipe, which allowed for easier, cheaper production and more elaborate forms. Glass remained an important material for containers because of its leak-proof qualities and water-tightness. In 1700, the first commercial glass factory in England was churning out 3 million bottles each year. Still, each was hand-blown and the process was labor intensive until the first fully automatic glass bottle-blowing machine was designed in the United States in 1903.

THE MARCH TOWARD FOOD PRESERVATION

If the adage "necessity is the mother of invention" were ever true, it would certainly apply to packaging. All packaging is produced to meet a need, of course, but the greater the need, the more energetic the response. In 1795, Napoleon Bonaparte found his armies stretched thin and far-flung, difficult to resupply.

Napolean offered a reward of 12,000 francs to anyone who could develop a safe, reliable method of preserving food for his troops. Answering the call was a Parisian chef named Nicholas Appert, who, in 1809, found that food sealed in glass containers and sterilized by heating would remain safe to eat for long periods. In 1810, Peter Durand, of Britain, received a patent on tin-plated iron containers dubbed "cans"—the first safe, sealed, cylindrical canisters for food.

As with pottery and stone vessels before them, these metal cans were completely opaque. Manufacturers were faced with the problem of communicating the cans' contents to the public, especially since the new process continued to grow in popularity. The next twenty years saw everything from meats to cookies to matches to tooth powders distributed in cans. In addition to paper labels and tags, methods were devised to print the cans' contents directly onto the metal exteriors. By the 1860s, printed metal cans and tins were also being produced in the United States. At the same time, European and American manufacturers were putting another material to use. An inexpensive substance called cardboard had been invented more than two hundred years earlier by Chinese papermakers. Western companies found that the material was rigid enough for packaging and transporting goods, with a surface that allowed for the evolving printing processes to label and decorate them. The oldest existing cardboard box package design was produced in Germany for a board game called "The Game of Besieging," in 1817.

Still, paper and cardboard were relative luxuries. This is because all paper was made by hand from rag pulp. Adding more stress to the industry was the fact that bleaching technology was nonexistent; only white rag pulp could be used to make white paper, which came primarily from Europe. Importing paper from Europe to the United States was an expensive proposition until techniques were developed to make paper not from rag, but from the pulp of wood and straw, both of which were plentiful in America. That development, coupled with the invention of papermaking machinery, quickly positioned America as the world's leading producer and consumer of paper and cardboard. Soon, paper labels on bottles, cans, cartons, and even wooden crates were the standard.

figure |1-5|

Early metal cans had hand-soldered seams and were filled through a small hole on top that was sealed after heating.

The Industrial Revolution brought sweeping changes across the entire spectrum of human experience. Mechanization flourished and introduced technological advances in all areas of commerce, including manufacturing and packaging. Paper grocery bags were already being used by grocers who would sift individual sales of flour, cereals, and other bulk items from larger sacks or barrels into smaller bags for customers. The invention of machines capable of sewing the ends of reinforced paper bags made the prepackaging of specified quantities of goods possible. Hand in hand with the changing face of packing, the printing industry, too, was going through a dramatic evolution. The new, better-quality papers allowed for improvements in the craft. In 1798, a printmaker named Alois Senefelder, frustrated by the high cost of copper engraving plates, invented the process of lithography—literally, "stone writing"—when he discovered that much cheaper stone plates could be marked with a greasy wax, moistened, and the ink applied to the plate would resist the water and adhere to the wax. Clean impressions of the design could then be made when paper was pressed against the stone. Senefelder and other printers continued to refine the process. Joseph Niepce, a French scientist, successfully produced the world's first photograph in 1826; by 1855, the two technologies merged when a French chemist named Alphonse Louis Poitevin coated a stone litho plate with light-sensitive chemicals and created photolithography, allowing photographic reproduction on a mass scale. For the first time, highly detailed and colorful images could be printed at very low cost, and manufacturers lost no time in putting them to full use.

Soon everything from fancy hatboxes to wooden crates of produce was adorned with elaborate and colorful labeling.

It was a logical step to combine lithographic printing with the sturdy packing material of cardboard. The surface readily accepted direct printing or the application of paper labels. Lightweight, sturdy, and easy to stack in warehouses or stand in shop displays, the cardboard box was quickly becoming accepted by both producers and consumers. Despite the obvious advances, problems remained. Issues of labor and storage tempered the growing popularity of cardboard packaging. Each box had to be hand-cut, glued, and folded. And once assembled, these boxes required so much space to warehouse that it was difficult to prepare them in truly useful quantities.

figure |1-6|

Brooklyn printer and bag maker Robert Gair.

THE BOX

In 1879, a Brooklyn printer and paper-bag maker named Robert Gair was printing an order of seed bags when a metal rule normally used to crease the bags inadvertently slipped in position and cut cleanly through the paper. Gair looked past the accident and explored its possibilities: he formed the idea that cardboard or paperboard could be creased by dull dies and cut by sharp dies in a single operation, giving birth to the ready-to-assemble folding carton. Boxes could then be printed, cut and creased, shipped or stored flat, and assembled easily. A seemingly simple concept, it nevertheless radically changed the face of packaging, making cardboard boxes and cartons economical, versatile, and the package of choice for a huge number of products from the nineteenth century to today. Gair went on to found a paper and packaging empire. Many buildings and warehouses in New York still bear his name.

With the ability to create inexpensive packaging for their products, manufacturers found themselves actively vying for the attention—and spending dollars—of an increasingly image-savvy public. In the late 1800s and early 1900s, most home goods such as sugar, flour, salt, and soap were still shipped in bulk to stores and shops and dispensed into smaller containers for individual sales. The opportunity existed for unscrupulous wholesalers to deliver inferior or

Photos by Rachelle Bowden (www.rachelleb.com)

figure |1-7|

Many buildings in New York still bear the name of Robert Gair, inventor of the folding cardboard box.

even unsanitary or adulterated products. Moreover, shopkeepers could sometimes be accused of short-weighing the dispensed items. We've all heard stories of "the grocer with the heavy thumb," referring to dishonest or inaccurate scales and measurements by retailers. With packaging, however, manufacturers could proclaim their products "100% pure," "sealed for freshness," or "satisfaction guaranteed"; they came preweighed, premeasured, easy to identify, and convenient to carry home. Consumers were encouraged to recognize a favorite brand and trust the promises of the packaging even more than the word of the familiar grocer. Packing was quickly becoming replaced by packaging, so much so that shoppers were asking less and less for "oatmeal" or "crackers," and more and more for "Quaker Oats" and "Uneeda Biscuits." Brand recognition and loyalty was reinforced by buyer experience, word of mouth, and a surge in the fledgling industry of advertising. The public saw and read about products in magazines, newspapers—even painted on the sides of buildings—and learned to ask for them by name or distinguish them from the others on a grocery shelf. In a way, packaging had become inseparable from the product itself. By 1930, national advertising strategies, employing the media of both print ads and radio commercials, had made individual, brand-name packaging the norm.

As packages became more common, many companies realized the value of communication in their design. Henry Parsons Crowell, a founder of Quaker Oats Company, concluded that shoppers would choose his product over others if the package was more communicative and informative. Crowell included cooking instructions, assurances of purity, and even recipes on the cardboard boxes to inform and attract buyers. Other oat and grain companies followed suit. To remain ahead of the field, Crowell had his packages reproduce more elaborate recipes, including those for bread, pudding, and baby food in addition to the familiar oatmeal cereal. In only a few years, he (and his competitors) had transformed a product that, until then, was seen mostly as feed for horses into a household staple, and the full-color logo of the Quaker Oats man, fashioned after Philadelphia's famous statue of William Penn, became a common sight in American pantries and cupboards.

Plastics and Polymers

While we often think of plastic as the newcomer of the packaging field, industry has been using organic polymers for hundreds of years. Waxes and shellacs are forms of these early "plastics," so called because of their malleability or "plasticity." The natural polymer rubber, made from the sap of rubber trees, was extensively used by the early 1800s. It was

Courtesy of Quaker

figure |1-8|

Quaker Oats sold prepackaged cereal and changed the way Americans shopped.

discovered that the addition of sulfur to natural rubber improved its properties, making it less sticky. In 1839, the American inventor Charles Goodyear found that heating the sulfur-rubber mix made the material stronger, more elastic, and less susceptible to abrasion. This process, known as vulcanization, helped make rubber a versatile material of industry.

Just a few years later, in 1862, the Englishman Alexander Parkes developed a synthetic substitute for ivory, which he called "Parkesine"—a cellulose and nitric acid-based substance that could be molded and shaped when heated. The American inventor John Wesley Hyatt improved the material by adding camphor and marketed it under the name "celluloid" in 1863. The new material continued to develop and find more applications from uses in artificial teeth and billiard balls to man-made silks that became known as "rayon." Rayon became a popular fabric from the 1930s to today, and can be produced in the form of a transparent sheet known as "cellophane."

By the mid-1930s, companies throughout the United States and Europe were producing various plastics such as acrylic and polyethylene, which were found to be excellent materials for packaging because of their lightweight natures and air-tight qualities. Today, polyethylene plastics are used to produce a broad range of packaging including beverage containers, processed-food packages, detergent bottles, plastic bags, and margarine tubs. Its cousin, polystyrene, is the material generally used in egg cartons, fast-food containers, and compact disc jewel cases. So prevalent is plastic in today's packaging that a recent study by the UK Plastics Industry found packaging claiming 36 percent—by far the largest segment—of the total plastics market, and making up 30 percent of all packaging.

From Containers to Communicators

With Quaker Oats, Uneeda crackers, and other widely "branded" goods—products distributed with the promise of consistency and excellence that took full advantage of strong visual graphics and copywriting—the art of package design moved from a technological or structural one to an art of aesthetics. And like all art forms, packaging found itself directly influenced by the prevalent styles and attitudes of the popular culture of the time. The packages of the early 1900s were adorned with the ornate scrolls, borders, and romantic scenes of the Art Nouveau period. In reaction to the growing industrialization they

figure │1-9│

Alexander Parkes patented his plastic "Parkesine" in 1862.

figure │1-10│

JOB cigarettes used the organic, ornate artwork of Alphonse Mucha to appeal to its audience.

saw around them, visual artists turned to the simplicity and beauty they associated with earlier times. The movement spread quickly across Europe and the United States and worked its way not only into painting and sculpture, but into the other visual arts as well, including architecture, furniture design, ceramics, and graphic design. Frequent themes were decorative stylizations of plant forms, flowing cloths, and intricate decorative patterns. Alphonse Mucha, a Czech graphic designer working in Paris, created many designs during this period, including signature pieces for JOB cigarette papers and others.

figure |1-11|

Many packages of the Art Nouveau period (1890–1920) depicted elongated, stylized figures and decorative borders, such as this cardboard box of Schrafft's chocolates.

By the mid-1920s, the typography of the Art Deco period gave a visual voice to post–World War I society. In a way not seen before, type designers were not only reflecting the new world around them, but conspicuously helping to shape it. Bold and geometric, typography of this Modernist period sought to capture the inventive vibrancy of the Jazz Age. Consumerism flourished, and advertising and package design were ready and willing to accommodate the stylistic trends of sleek, clean, streamlined fashion. Manufacturers were not only selling products, they were selling a lifestyle: packages mimicked the tall lines of skyscrapers and the opulence of ocean liners. Interestingly, the power of packages to communicate more than the product within, but also an attitude or sense of identity for the consumer, led to an ever-increasing array of package designs, each looking to attract another segment of the buying public. In the years of 1925–1930, the Palmolive Company produced no fewer than five different packages of talcum powder under separate names, each conveying its message to a different audience. The contents were the same, but the packages were the messengers, each holding out another promise. The package, in many cases, was the product.

© Watkins, Inc.

figure |1-12|

The Art Deco period of package design in the 1920s and 1930s saw, as one aspect, a craze of "Egyptomania." Ancient Egyptian motifs found their way into such modern products as talcum powder and cigarettes.

The discovery of King Tutankhamen's tomb in 1922, with all its artifacts and riches intact, led to a wave of "Egyptomania" in Western popular culture and the graphic arts. Tall, obelisk-like packages were adorned with slab-serif, "Egyptian" typefaces. Hieroglyphic motifs abounded, along with images of scarabs, sphinxes, and regal, stately cats. The craze ushered in numerous new typographic fonts and simplified color schemes.

Package design, as a field, was coming into its own, and was changing the way consumers and retailers interacted. Before, shoppers were happy with the limited choices they were offered, and looked to the grocer or shopkeeper to advise and guide them. Now, the products themselves were speaking to them, offering information, and assuring buyers that they'd made the right choice. In a very real sense, the salesperson was becoming obsolete; packages were already serving as salespeople, working around the clock, always ready and focused. This was not only a commercial adjustment, but a sociological transfer of power. As Richard B. Franken and Carroll B. Larabee put it in their 1928 book, *Packages That Sell:* "The display container is as much of a salesman as any flesh and blood clerk, and often more, for it works night and day for one product and emphasizes only those sales arguments which the manufacturer knows are best." Package design itself had become a topic of study, conversation, and significance.

figure |1-13|

As late as the 1900s, store shelves were organized more for the shopkeeper's convenience than for customers'.

The Package as Salesperson

While the 1920s and 30s led us past World War I, and through the Depression and Recovery, the 1940s found us weathering the storm of yet another World War. With so many able-bodied men and women called to duty, the local store was more hard-pressed for sales clerk personnel than ever. Fortunately, package design was quick to take up the slack. Already accustomed to the selling power of packaged goods, store owners allowed their establishments to become even more self-serviced than they had in the past, relying on the information included on packaging

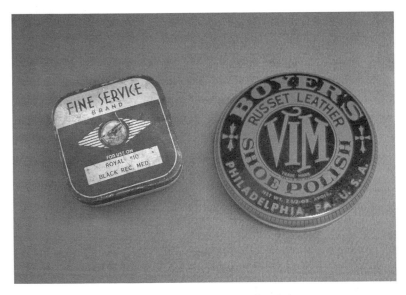

figure |1-14|

Tin was an economical choice of packaging in the '20s and '30s. Here, it's used for such everyday products as typewriter ribbons and shoe polish.

to answer the consumers' questions and make the sale. Copywriting for product packages evolved from extolling the content's attributes into full-fledged instruction for operation and uses. With minimal outside interaction, a shopper could go to the store, choose the correct product, and learn how to use or operate it when they arrived home, all from the packaging itself. It was apparent early on that the packaging of a product could do as much or more for its perception by consumers than could shop owners, clerks, or salespeople. One pioneer of the study of packages and the messages they send was Louis Cheskin. Cheskin conducted experiments in the way people perceive packages and their contents. In his most famous study, Cheskin placed identical products into two packages—one having circles on the outside of the package and one having triangles. He didn't ask his subjects any questions about the packages, but had them rate the quality of the products. The participants overwhelmingly rated the products packaged with the circles above the same product packaged with triangles. Cheskin repeated the experiment over and over again, each time with the same results. His research indicated that a package's design had a direct influence on the consumer's judgment of the product inside. Working as a consultant in the 1950s, he advised Betty Crocker to add the graphic image of a spoon to their logo. Sales almost doubled in under a year.

Similar experiments conducted by Cheskin and other marketing psychologists suggest that we are influenced by every aspect of package design—size, shape, color, typography, packaging material—far more than we are ever aware. Each choice a designer makes when creating a package will impact its effectiveness in ways that go far beyond the aesthetics.

Digital Design

The 1980s saw the advent of a new set of tools and technologies that changed the way graphic artists and package designers worked. Apple Computers introduced the Macintosh computer, the first computer to combine graphics, digital typesetting, and high-resolution output. Its advantage was that art appeared on the computer screen exactly as it would print, and this "what you see is what you get" feature set it apart from the earlier methods of typesetting and production work. Design ideas could also be manipulated and rearranged quickly and easily, allowing for exploration and revision. A variety of software has grown across various computer platforms and operating systems; from graphic design, digital imaging, and advanced typography to Auto-CAD (computer aided drawing) that allows artists to create 3-D renderings of their designs before they ever produce a mockup, the use of digital technology brought more freedom to visual artists, pushing limitations aside and seeking new and innovative package design solutions.

figure |1-15|

The Digital Revolution changed many aspects of life, from the way we communicated to the way we worked, and how graphic artists applied their art.

18,000 BC

1630 AD

18,000 BC-1630 AD

100,000 years ago

Natural containers found and modified from animal skins, gourds, leaves

18,000 BC
Basket weaving, leather bottles are used for storage

6000 BC
Hand-formed pottery is developed in Japan and the Mediterranean

3000 BC
Earliest examples of wooden boxes Canopic jars are used in Egyptian funereal preparation Papyrus is processed into flat writing surface

1500 BC
Potter's wheel is invented

1000 BC
Glass blowing technique introduced by Phoenicians

1 AD
First true paper invented in China

1040
Movable type printing invented in Germany

1100
First paper arrives in Europe from China

1450
Gutenberg invents movable type in Germany

1630
First paper bags used in commerce

figure |1-16|

This timeline traces the history of packing and packaging.

figure |1-17|

Old apothacary jars and bottles become artifacts of package design.

So, what does all this mean for the student of packaging? The designer today has a greater option of tools, technologies, and packaging materials than ever before. Glass, metal, cardboard, paper, and plastic all play important roles as packaging substrates, and offer a broad spectrum of choices to address both the structural and creative concerns of the package designer. Having a useful, working knowledge of these materials and techniques will make your decisions informed, insightful, and communicative.

1700 AD   1991 AD

1700 AD–1991 AD

1700
First commercial glass factory in England

1795
Napoleon Bonaparte offers prize for food preservation

1798
Alois Senefelder invents lithographic printing

1810
Peter Durand creates system for tin-plated cans of food

1817
"The Game of Besieging" is packaged in a cardboard box

1839
Charles Goodyear refines process of 'vulcanization' of rubber

1855
Photolithography and offset printing invented

1860
Alexander Parkes produces first synthetic plastic

1867
Paper is made from wood pulp

1879
Robert Gair invents folding cardboard packaging

1890
Corrugated cardboard is invented

1903
Corrugated cardboard boxes are used on a large scale

1922
Crimped-on air-tight seal for metal cans (making soldering of seals obsolete) allows for high-speed food canning

1933
Polythene invented in Britain

1940
Aerosols are first used

1960
The first tamper-resistant packaging is introduced

1980
Digital hardware and software for graphic design and packaging developed
Microwaveable food packages are developed

1991
Every food and beverage package sold in U.S. is redesigned to incorporate 'Nutrition Facts' information

SUMMING IT UP

The human need to pack and package is as old as civilization. The capability to grow and gather more food and resources than could be immediately used necessitated the development of means of storage.

Clearly, the communicative power and technology used to produce our containers has grown, but the function of a PET bottle carrying a high-energy sports drink is the same as the hollow gourd filled with spring water: to preserve, store, and transport a commodity for future use. Having an appreciation for the history and development of packing and packaging provides the designer of today with cultural, technological, and material reference points upon which to build.

PROFILE

Ian House

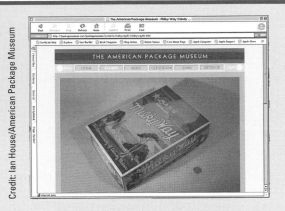

Ian House is curator of The American Package Museum, where specimens of twentieth-century American packaging are exhibited, preserved, and archived. House's interests in American history drive his involvement with the museum; he views commercial packages as important artifacts of our evolving society. "The history of package design," he explains, "provides us with a valuable archive of our cultural heritage and the development of our consumer society. If we study the thousands of branding icons that surround us every day and compare them to the designs from a hundred years ago, we'll learn a great deal about our American culture and ourselves as a people. Advertising iconography reflects our values during any given period of time."

Many visitors remark on the powerful memories they associate with the exhibits. "It proves true that the items are not simply irrelevant objects," House says. "They are items, seemingly mundane, that offer a profound emotional connection to the past."

An online version of the museum serves two purposes. Exhibits are more readily accessed, and by a greater number of visitors, than would otherwise be possible. Additionally, fragile pieces are photographed, recorded digitally, and made available to viewers while allowing the original artifact to be safely stored and protected, away from the harmful effects of light, moisture, or handling. "Our museum has many objectives: Primarily, we endeavor to preserve and display our exhibits using the most effective methods possible. It's our belief that these articles represent an important connection to our past and should be protected from any further physical degradation just like any other museum pieces." You can visit the online museum at ww.packagemuseum.com.

As a resource, the American Package Museum's website offers an interesting and informative look at familiar packaging icons for students of both cultural history and the graphic arts, generating over 36,000 hits a year. But its audience is not limited to those with academic interests. Numerous visitors are simply drawn to its exhibits by a sense of recognition and reminiscence, a sort of visual dialogue with the past. House isn't surprised. As he puts it, "Package design is primarily a communication medium." ∎

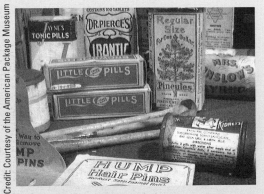

Packaging goes beyond the nostalgic and delves into the sociologic aspects of consumerism.

in review

1. Discuss the purposes of packages and containers. Why are they necessary, and how has the need for them changed as society evolved?

2. What is the difference between a container and a package? What common traits do they share?

3. Manufacturers have greater choices in packaging materials than ever before. What are some of the technological advances that have led to changes in packaging?

exercises

1. Nature provides many natural containers, such as gourds, bamboo, and seashells. Come up with a list of your own, naming at least five other natural containers. Find as many physical examples as you can.

2. Looking around the home, gather packages made from the five materials discussed in this chapter—clay, glass, paper or cardboard, metal, and plastic. Make a chart that lists the advantages and drawbacks of each material.

3. Research a product that has existed for a number of years. Examine how the packaging has transformed over the years and make notes of its evolution, including its packaging material, package color and shape, and typographic treatment.

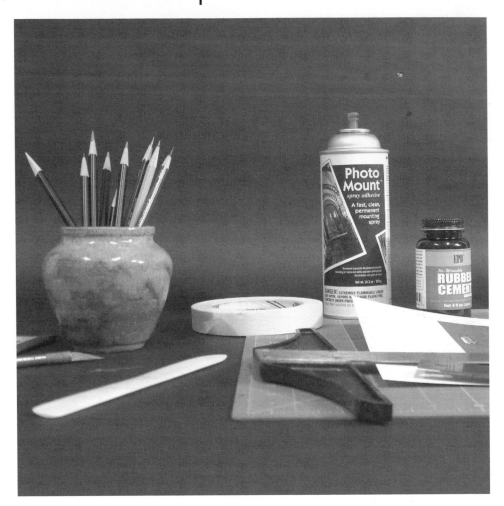

CHAPTER

"We must distinguish between the kind of constructions in which form and material have remained independent from each other, from those where form and material have become inseparable—only thus will we give justice to the work and derive from it a supreme kind of enjoyment."

Paul Valery, "Regards sur le Monde Actuel"

Chapter Objectives

Introduce some common tools for package designers

Recognize design paradigms in the world around us

Explore common packaging materials

Understand the basic forms of packaging

Introduction

The design of packaging requires not only a new set of hand skills for the graphic artist, from creative engineering to the mastering of mock-up construction, but a different way of thinking about a solution and presenting information. Package design, when it's effective, employs a complex hierarchy and flow of elements that

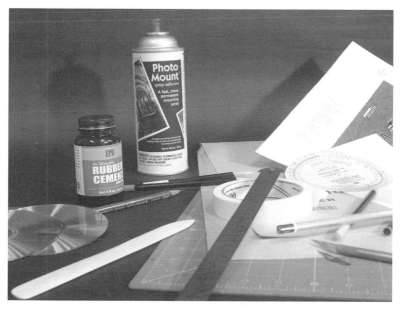

figure |2-1|

Proper tools—and the ability to use them—are essential for the package designer.

figure | 2-2 |

Bristol board is usually found in pads like this, available in standard sizes such as 8½" x 11", 11" x 14", and 14" x 20".

contrast with designing on a two-dimensional plane. In many ways, it's as distinct as the difference between painting a picture of a house and building a house.

THE TOOLS OF THE PACKAGE DESIGNER

Before starting to design a package, it's important to familiarize yourself with the basic toolbox you will need to produce your pieces. Start by taking a look at some of the traditional board tools designers use to create their 3-D mock-ups.

- **Bristol board.** Bristol board is a common substrate for creating 3-D package mock-ups and prototypes. A semi-rigid paper, Bristol is available in a variety of weights, or thicknesses. For most of your pieces, a good-quality, two-ply Bristol board will be ideal. It holds its form well, cuts and folds easily, and has a smooth surface to which you can apply graphics or other visual and textural elements. When a more substantial substrate is needed, you can choose three-ply Bristol or even glue two sheets together for added strength.

- **Tracing paper.** No good graphic designer should be caught without tracing paper. Thin and translucent, tracing paper provides a good surface for sketching, quickly redrawing and refining designs, tracing graphics such as logos or custom typography, mounting your work (I'll explain this later on in the chapter), and protecting flat work for presentation.

- **X-Acto or hobby knife.** The X-Acto knife is the perfect tool for making clean, precise cuts in most of the materials you will be using for package mock-ups. X-Acto knives are designed to hold replaceable blades, which are available in an array of shapes and styles. I've always been satisfied with the blade sold as No. 11—it's versatile with a very fine point, and cuts through media as thin as vellum and as thick as heavy cardboard. Handles also come in an assortment of styles, and it's fine to use the style that suits you best and feels most comfortable; the more natural the knife feels in your hand, the more accurately you will be able to use it.

- **Metal ruler.** You cannot do without a reliable metal ruler. The metal provides a straight, true edge for drawing, scoring, and cutting, and will not be damaged by

figure | 2-3 |

An X-Acto knife is indispensable when working in packaging.

an X-Acto blade. The same cannot be said for a plastic or wooden ruler. And metal rulers will be used throughout the composition process to determine measurements and proportions. Stainless steel rules will never rust, are not affected by humidity, and will serve you for years. If you choose a ruler with a cork backing, you won't be disappointed; these rulers will not slip when you are making delicate cuts or drawing lines with pen or pencil.

figure |2-4|

A metal ruler will be valuable not only in measuring, but as a straight edge while cutting.

- **Scoring tool.** Papers and boards are purchased as flat sheets, which is fine for two-dimensional design. But to re-form those flat sheets into packages, you will need to bend, fold, and assemble the piece into its 3-D shape. A scoring tool will make your life easier and your mock-ups more professional. The tool is used to create an indentation in the packaging flat along which a clean fold can be made. Many scoring tools are made of plastic, metal, or bone. If you are lucky, you will find one with several different scoring width options. In a pinch, I've even used a strong paper clip or a ballpoint pen in lieu of a scoring tool.

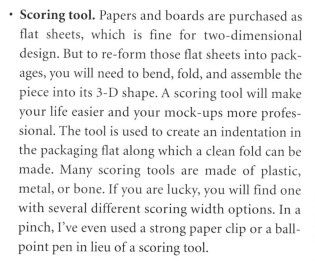

- **Cutting mat.** A cutting mat can be made of any material that will adequately protect your work surface and will not interfere with making a clean cut. Many students have found that scrap mat board or the chipboard backing of paper pads

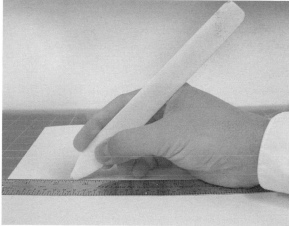

figure |2-5|

A scoring tool is used whenever folds in the paper or board are necessary.

(such as tracing paper or Bristol board) make good cutting mats. One problem with these is that each cut mars the surface, and after multiple cuts, you may find your cutting mat is no longer smooth and is, in fact, impeding your attempts to cut. The best, though more expensive, choice would be to invest in a "self-healing" rubber cutting mat; as the name suggests, these leave no surface inconsistencies even after multiple uses, and the easy "give" of the surface allows a sharp knife blade to glide through a cut without catching on the mat. These mats can be found through architectural drawing supply stores or at the local sewing or hobby shop, since they are often used by crafters for cutting fabric.

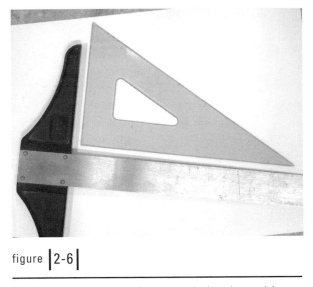

figure |2-6|

The T-square and drafting triangles are designed to work in harmony with each other.

- **T-square.** A T-square is a tool commonly used in drafting, architectural, or technical drawing. It gets its name from its two parts: a long, rectangular bar with another, shorter head attached perpendicular to the bar, forming the shape of a "T." Used properly, a T-square will allow a designer to draw any number of parallel, horizontal lines on board or paper.
- **Drafting triangles.** You will need at least two large drafting triangles. Triangles, typically made of plastic or metal, are used in conjunction with the T-square to draw vertical or angular lines. The most common triangles are the 45–45–90 and the 30–60–90. The first will enable you to draw, in relation to the T-square, lines at true 45-degree and 90-degree angles; the second will allow you to draw 30-degree, 60-degree, or 90-degree angles. These will be useful when determining cuts, folds, and surface divisions for your packaging. Another useful tool is the adjustable triangle. Adjustable triangles are made of two separate parts connected by a sliding gauge, making it possible to draw lines at any desired angle. These are a great addition to your supply list, but should not be chosen to replace the 45–45–90 or 30–60–90 triangles.
- **Adhesives.** For the package designer, adhesives take several forms. Every designer will want to have a high-quality rubber cement on hand. Find a brand you're comfortable with, but be sure it's acid-free and thin enough to be workable. Thick or lumpy rubber cement will, in every case, lead to messy and uneven work. Another type of glue that is very useful in producing mock-ups is spray adhesive. Spray adhesive is, essentially, rubber cement in aerosol form. It comes in two types, each serving a different function. Repositionable spray adhesive works just as it sounds: it will adequately glue a project together, and if necessary, it will allow the two pieces to be separated and repositioned. Because it has this feature, you should be aware that it is not intended to create a permanent bond. It will generally last long enough to photograph a mock-up or give a presentation, but when looking for something more archival, you might consider a permanent spray adhesive, often marketed under the category of Photo Mount. With either choice, these sprays take some practice to apply neatly and correctly, but once you have the hang of them, they can make your work fast and neat. Other adhesives you will need include common paper glue, school-quality glue-stick, double-sided tapes, masking tape, and contact cement.
- **Rubber cement pickup.** A rubber cement pickup is a small square of crepe rubber used to clean up excess rubber cement that has dried on your work. Rubber cement can be removed by rubbing it from the paper with your fingers, but the pickup does this without getting any oils or dirt on your finished work.

- **Acetate.** If you are designing a package with a window that shows the product within but you still want the object to be completely contained, an acetate covering over the die cut window is a good option. Acetate film can be purchased in a wide range of colors and weights, from very thin and flimsy to thick and rigid. Acetate can be scored, cut, and folded similarly to paper or Bristol board, and some types can even be fed through a laser or ink jet printer.

- **Mounting board.** Mounting board, or mat board, is cardboard made from several layers of thinner board glued together, with the two outer layers of a higher quality than the inner layers. Mounting board is typically $\frac{1}{16}$th of an inch thick, and can be purchased in black, white, or almost any color. It's rigid and flat, and its strength lends itself to providing a clean background for flat work that can be held, passed around a table, or displayed on an easel, making it invaluable for client presentations. You may also find yourself using mounting board as supplemental reinforcement to your packaging mock-ups when extra strength is called for, and as a base material when designing point-of-purchase displays.

- **Additional supplies:** Each designer will also find the need for many other common art supplies, and if you have an idea of some of the more common things to keep on hand, you will be better prepared to work. Scissors, pens and pencils, a variety of markers—broad and fine point—in several colors, a decent set of color pencils, construction paper, Pantone Color guide, an artists' proportion wheel (further description of the proportion wheel's use will be provided), and access to a graphics-equipped computer (with appropriate software and media to save your work, such as ZIP disks, CDs, or the newer USB flash drives now available) will all be necessary as you proceed.

figure **2-7**

The package designer's toolbox. These are some of the standard supplies necessary to produce quality work and clean, professional package comps.

WORKING WITH PACKAGING MATERIALS AND TOOLS

Now that you've assembled the supplies to produce packaging mock-ups, there are some aspects of working with those elements that need to be addressed. You already know how to handle your pens, pencils, sketch paper, and other basic drawing media. When you are working three-dimensionally, it's essential to have an understanding of the specific characteristics of the materials you will be working with so that you can make intelligent, thoughtful, and practical choices in form and function. You will be folding, cutting, bending, and transforming the packaging materials to fit your needs. The following techniques will help you to accomplish those tasks easily, cleanly, and professionally.

Cutting with an X-Acto knife

The X-Acto knife is one of the most fundamental tools of graphic designers of any ilk, but when you are producing 3-D comps, the knife is indispensable. If you know how to properly use the tool, all of your production work will benefit.

The first thing to know: the X-Acto is extremely sharp and, therefore, care must be taken when using it. That care begins with the idea that a new, sharp blade will cut more cleanly and safely than an old, dull blade. It just makes sense that the harder you have to pull a knife through your medium, the more you must trade control for power. X-Acto blades are very inexpensive, and there is really no excuse for attempting to employ a blade when it's no longer sharp or effective. CHANGE YOUR BLADES OFTEN.

figure |2-8|

Properly holding the knife will lead to accurate and safe cuts, whether cutting tracing paper or mat board.

You should hold the X-Acto as you would a pencil. It should feel comfortable in your hand and easy to control. Do not grasp the knife like it's a screwdriver or garden trowel—you will be using it with precision, not force. It's also important, particularly when your substrate is thick enough that it requires more than one pass with the blade, to keep these things in mind: you must try to position the blade so that it is ALWAYS cutting at the same angle, and you must not allow your cutting guide (such as a T-square or metal ruler) to move until the cut is completed (see Figure 2-8). Failing to remember these points when using the knife will result in rough or inaccurate cuts. One cannot overemphasize the benefits of practicing safe, clean cutting techniques.

Scoring

At certain points in your package construction, you'll find that it's preferable to fold rather than to cut the board. To make the board fold exactly where you've determined, you must first score—or crease—the board. There are two different ways to score a piece of cardboard. First, a designer may use a sharp blade to cut the first few layers of fiber (see Figure 2-9), without cutting all the way through the board. Care must be taken that you do not slice completely through your paper, even in small sections along the crease. Advantages to this knife method include speed (it is a very quick and easy way to score paper or board) and precision (a score made by this technique will result in a crisp, well-defined fold). There are several drawbacks,

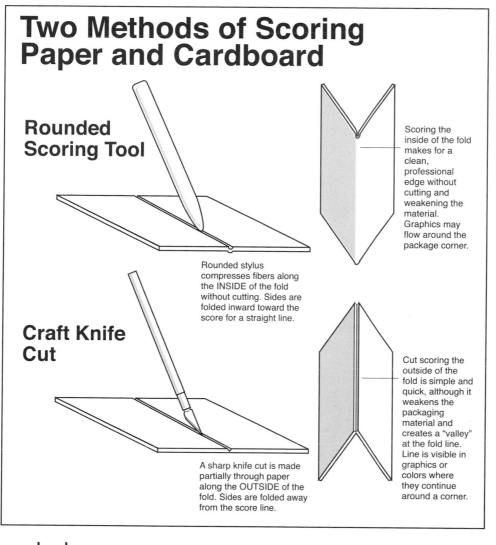

Two Methods of Scoring Paper and Cardboard

Rounded Scoring Tool

Scoring the inside of the fold makes for a clean, professional edge without cutting and weakening the material. Graphics may flow around the package corner.

Rounded stylus compresses fibers along the INSIDE of the fold without cutting. Sides are folded inward toward the score for a straight line.

Craft Knife Cut

Cut scoring the outside of the fold is simple and quick, although it weakens the packaging material and creates a "valley" at the fold line. Line is visible in graphics or colors where they continue around a corner.

A sharp knife cut is made partially through paper along the OUTSIDE of the fold. Sides are folded away from the score line.

figure | 2-9 |

The two methods of scoring paperboard. Using a blade will be fast and crisp, but will result in a weaker fold and a "valley" in the board surface. Compressing the board is more time-consuming, but usually a preferred technique.

however, to this approach that should be noted. Cutting through several layers of fiber in the board will obviously weaken the material. If the mock-up is likely to be handled by the client or other designers, the weakened fold could lead to a tear at the seam. Additionally, the resulting valley in the paper or board, as illustrated, will reveal an unsightly line in your surface graphics, which is likely to collect dirt, glue, and oils from your hand in a very short time. The preferable way of scoring paper or board for a fold is by compressing, rather than cutting, the fibers along the desired fold line. This is achieved by using a scoring tool and running it with some pressure along the fold (see Figure 2-9). First, align your metal ruler on the inside surface of the fold you want to make. If necessary, use a light table (a tabletop surface of glass or Plexiglas with fluorescent lights beneath it that enable you to see through thin to moderately thick paper or board) to place a straight edge along the line you wish to score. Holding the scoring tool firmly, pull it all the way through the line you plan to fold, applying firm, even pressure. By compressing the paper fibers along the ruler, you will find that you can simply bend the substrate inward toward the score to make a clean fold. As with many of the new skills you'll be learning in this book, practice will lead to proficiency; attempt them over and over again on scrap material until you have a confident feel for the procedure.

Rubber Cement

Still another skill you should familiarize yourself with before attempting mock-ups is the application of adhesives. There are various points in which you will need to use adhesives in packaging, and each has its own specific glue and method of application. First, we'll discuss the use of rubber cement, since it's the most common adhesive used in graphic design for comps, mock-ups, and presentations. At the outset, you should know that rubber cement falls under the category of contact cement—that is, it is a glue that's designed to stick to itself. As such, the proper application of rubber cement means that it is to be spread across BOTH SURFACES to be joined. Therefore, the more smoothly and evenly the cement is spread, the greater the surface area of adhesion. Once both surfaces have been coated with a thin layer of rubber cement, any contact between the two pieces will bond them together, and trying to reposition them will almost certainly mar or even destroy your work. A simple step here will enable you to easily and accurately align and position the two pieces of work. Lay the bottom piece of work glue side up on your work surface. Take two sheets of tracing paper, and place them over the bottom section of work, overlapping them by at least half an inch in the center. You must use tracing paper large enough to completely cover the area of glue; if necessary, use more than two, overlapping them all. If you have allowed the rubber cement to dry completely, the tracing paper will not stick to the glue, which will allow you to remove them later. Next, place your second piece to be adhered glue side down on top of the tracing paper. This configuration should now have the two glue-coated sides facing each other with tracing paper separating them. You can now position the top piece exactly where you want it to align correctly with the bottom piece. Once it is in place, hold it along the left edge so that it will not move, and pull out the piece of tracing paper on the right. Gently push the two glued surfaces together. Now, remove the piece of tracing paper from the left side. For added protection of your work, it's a good idea to then lay the pieces of tracing paper over the work and press over the entire surface to make complete contact of the cemented pieces. With a rubber cement pickup,

figure | 2-10 |

Placing two pieces of tracing paper overlapped in the center and between the two surfaces to be cemented allows for accurate positioning. With a rubber cement pickup, clean the excess rubber cement from the work.

you can clean up any excess rubber cement that has dried outside the gluing area. This method of rubber cementing pieces together sounds complicated, but it's actually simple and fast once you practice it, and it will lead to the very best bond. You can use this technique when gluing printed graphics to Bristol board for mock-ups, gluing paper to paper, or when gluing paper to mounting board for presentations.

Using the T-square and Triangles

Regardless of how much design work is produced digitally by using a computer and software, every graphic artist should be familiar with the proper use of a T-square and triangles, particularly when creating presentation boards, 3-D mock-ups, and surface graphics that use different media or sections pieced together.

The T-square and triangles enable you to draw parallel, perpendicular, and diagonal lines at a variety of specific angles with ease and precision, but only if they are used properly. Your work surface, such as a drawing board or a tabletop, should have a straight edge along one side to align the T-square head. Pick one edge of your work surface (for most artists, this is the left edge) and one edge only; this will become the constant, the reference edge for all the other lines you will be drawing with the drafting tools. Place the head of the T-square tightly and squarely against this edge. As you slide the T-square along your reference edge, the horizontal bar should be moving vertically in a straight line. If you tape a piece of paper to your drawing table (you tape it to keep it from moving—even slightly—and becoming misaligned) and place the T-square against your reference edge, you can draw a horizontal line along the bar. Slide the square up two or three inches and draw another line; these two lines should be parallel to each other. In fact, every line you draw along the square's horizontal bar should be

parallel to the others. You can test this by drawing a few horizontal lines, and then moving the square back to the first. If you've controlled the T-square correctly, the bar should line up perfectly with the first line, and each successive line, drawn. Practice this until you can consistently produce straight, parallel lines with the T-square.

Drafting triangles are used in combination with the T-square to draw vertical and diagonal lines. The triangle should always be placed flat against the straight edge of the square's bar. With the 45–45–90 triangle, you can produce lines of 45 degrees, 90 degrees, and 135 degrees. The 30–60–90 triangle will give you angles of 30 degrees, 60 degrees, 90 degrees, 120 degrees, and 150 degrees. And if you use the triangles together, it's possible to form angles in fifteen-degree increments from 0 to 180 (Figure 2-11).

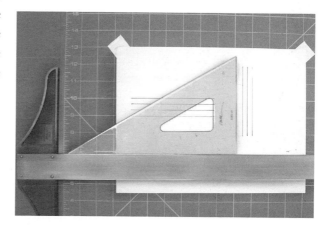

figure |2-11|

Proper use of the T-square and triangles makes it possible to draw and cut horizontal, vertical, and diagonal lines accurately. The head of the T-square must always be tight against the reference edge of the board or table.

Following a 2-D Pattern for a 3-D Form

Developing a firm understanding of two-dimensional patterns is of great importance to the package designer. Designs are usually concepted in sketch form—first roughly, then in more detail—as dimensional, or plan, drawings. Once certain decisions are made, such as the overall size and shape of the package and how and where it will open, the package must be engineered to function, to protect the product, and to be produced as easily and efficiently as possible. Computer designs are perfected and completed and applied to digital templates. This means that while the package designer is working two-dimensionally, he or she must constantly be thinking three-dimensionally, and while working three-dimensionally, must always be cognizant of the two-dimensional ramifications. It's a continuous back-and-forth.

All of this sounds intimidating. Mastering the diverse disciplines of drawing, typography, design and, on top of that, engineering as well? Fortunately, it's all a lot more manageable than it may seem. Just as a student of music starts out playing scales (over and over and over) and eventually learns to manipulate those scales, rearranging the notes to create music, the package designer familiarizes him or herself with the basic forms and their construction, then modifies these patterns to make them suitable to particular products, more functional and unique. Soon, it becomes second nature to look at a package and understand, after just a few seconds, its basic 2-D pattern. But before the musician improvises, there is that time playing scales.

As a warm-up—a sort of "five-finger exercise"—let's follow a basic cube construction, from rough sketches through its refined pattern and on to a 3-D model. First, it's best to define the problem. In this case, we'll be designing a $2^1/_2$-inch six-sided box. There are many ways to arrange the panels, any additional flaps that might be necessary, and methods

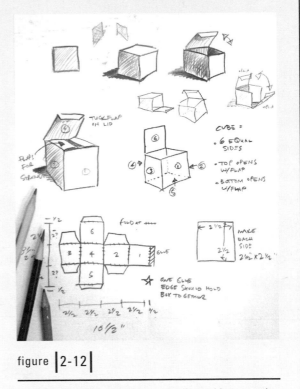

figure | 2-12 |

The cube is sketched with several different ideas, mostly pertaining to how the box will open. The sides are numbered and a basic layout is tried.

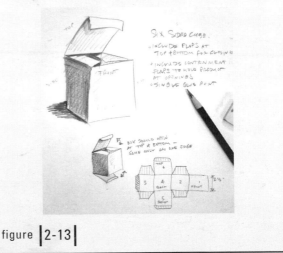

figure | 2-13 |

The drawing is developed further. Here, it's been determined that the cube will open at both top and bottom. A single glue tab will be required to hold the box together, with the additional flaps adding rigidity to the top and bottom as they tuck to close.

of opening the box, so it's a good idea to begin with some very quick sketches. While sketching, try to explore some different ways to approach the problem.

Good drawing skills are helpful here. The ability to draw the cube in perspective, at least fairly well, makes it possible to envision the box as a 3-D form before it's ever constructed. It also makes it easier to visualize where panels will meet, how they will fold, and to determine specific glue points for the model.

Once the box has been carefully planned in pencil, a precise flat pattern can be made. This can be done on the drawing board with a T-square and triangles, or in a computer graphics application.

Attention must be paid to the accurate measurements of the panels, flaps, and glue tabs.

This example is all about form and technique, and not directly about the visual surface. We'll discuss organization of information and applying surface graphics to the package in the next chapter. ■

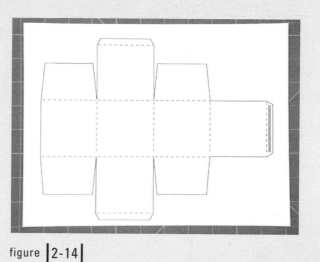

figure |2-14|

With either traditional drafting tools or computer software, an accurate 2-D pattern for the box is drawn. All flaps and glue tabs must be included at this stage to construct the box from a single piece of paper or Bristol board.

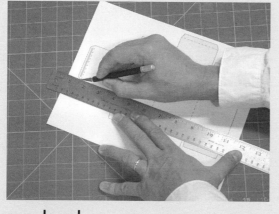

figure |2-15|

The print is cut and scored.

figure |2-16|

The assembled cube.

PROFILE

Dustin Commer

© Dustin Commer, LPG Design

In Wichita's competitive design market—there are over twenty local full-service design studios in the Kansas town of under 500,000 people—designer Dustin Commer has found a home and a career at LPG Design, where he has worked for over six years. "LPG Design has been able to go outside of Wichita for some accounts, and we have been very successful doing so," Commer says. "Many of our clients come to us for brand identity, a new look for an invention they're trying to sell, or a product headed for Wal-Mart. Packaging is our expertise, but we don't limit ourselves to just that."

But "just that" is what drew Commer to the field. "When I was studying to become a designer, I chose the direction I felt the most comfortable in—dimensional packaging. I loved collecting them, taking complicated pieces apart, discovering how different materials fold and bend, then designing them on my own."

For inspiration, he looks to the antique graphics he collects, "from cigarette tins to soap boxes, movie posters to vintage ads in magazines such as *Boy's Life* and *National Geographic*." He studies these examples from the past not to copy, but to carry on. As Commer puts it, "I simply love to reintroduce my favorite and most memorable looks,

FORM FOLLOWS FUNCTION

There's an old adage in art that says, "form follows function," meaning, of course, that the desired *function* of an object must logically have an impact on the *form* that object will take. For example, let's say we want to design a container for brewing and serving hot tea. This function—the *intent* of the piece—will quickly dictate certain constraints right off the bat. Materials will need to be waterproof and capable of withstanding the heat of the water. So immediately, we can begin to include some possible materials for consideration and exclude others. Other concerns to address: How will the tea and water enter the container? How will the tea be poured from the container once brewed? Obviously, the function of the container will lead to the form's inclusion of openings or spouts, logically placed, if it is to be useful. It's no accident or mere coincidence that the *function* of the together with my own interpretation, and appropriately apply them to each product or organization I design for."

Over the course of his career, Dustin has seen the Internet affect an influence over all aspects of current design, packaging being no exception. "Icons or 'bugs' have become a major part of design today," he says. "On the 'net, you click on a bug to go to a link, or it bullets an important point; most packaging today will also have a clearly recognizable icon next to copy in order to generate interest and an association, just as they do on the Internet."

Other trends he sees: "Creating a package that is sleek, better displays the product, and is eye catching with the most important information quickly recognizable. Additionally, the more savvy and skeptical consumer will notice the proper use of color for the product, and more detailed information.

"Always think of each panel of the package as a separate page. Create a package that relates to the product, and use relative elements of the product as a starting point for the design.

"As a designer," Commer continues, "I purchase some products just because the packaging is really cool. I'm drawn to more artful packaging . . . packaging that incorporates lots of fun and creative design. I also buy products with rather unique packaging structures. I'm drawn to products that use metal for packaging or a rare die cut or fold (I usually display well-designed packaging in my office or at home for inspiration).

"There is a degree of natural talent, experience, and knowledge of medium and tools that is required to be able to produce a quality 3-D piece. The designer has to understand the levels of depth and perspective of objects and understand all the curves, the shadows, the changes in color, the glare and the 'movement' of the object."

LPG Design, in Wichita, Kansas, is an award-winning creative and marketing communications studio. It produces private labeling, sales kits, logo designs, packaging, and point-of-purchase displays and Web site design. Visit LPG Design on the Web at www.lpgdesign.com. ■

teapot has led to a generally consistent expression of its *form* that crosses oceans, cultures, and aesthetic tastes. Likewise, when designing a package, its primary functions must be understood at the outset. The purpose of any package, first and foremost, is as a container and protector for the product within. Every aesthetic, then, comes second to this list of standards: Does this package hold the product? Will the package stay together and protect the product through shipping, shelf display, and purchase? And does the structure make sense for the product, client, and intended audience? No matter how pretty the graphics or typography, how innovative or creative the package's shape and appearance, if it does not meet the preceding criteria, it will not be a successful solution to the problem. Interestingly, most products can be contained within a rather simple assortment of structures, although each structure will allow for an almost infinite number of deviations and "variations on a theme." These basic structures include the six-sided box (the vast majority of packages fall into this category, for reasons we'll examine later), the pyramid (which can

figure |2-18|

Different teapots from around the world share a common understanding of "form follows function."

figure |2-17|

Architect and designer Louis Sullivan.

have any number of sides, though typically have three or four sides and a base), the cone—essentially a rounded pyramid—and the cylinder. To become acquainted with the construction of 3-D packaging structures, it's best to begin by analyzing these basic forms.

The observant designer will see examples of each of these forms many times each day, occurring both naturally and in the man-made world. Each grain of salt takes on the shape of a cube, which can be seen under magnification. This form is so common, it's used in applications—large and small—from making bricks, buildings, and bookcases, to children's blocks.

"It is the pervading law of all things organic . . . of all true manifestations of the head, of the heart, of the soul, that life is recognizable in its expression, that form ever follows function."

Louis Sullivan

Recognizing Paradigms

The dictionary gives these definitions for the word *paradigm:*

1. a typical example of something; 2. an example that serves as a pattern or model for something, especially one that forms the basis of a methodology or theory.

We are surrounded by packaging paradigms. Everywhere we look, we can find examples and utilizations of the basic forms most often used in package design. If a designer is on the lookout for these paradigms, appropriate form choices and innovative applications can be found—sometimes where least expected. Several examples of the cube were given a

figure |2-19|

Every day, designers look to seemingly incongruous sources to find the answers to their problems.

moment ago. But what use are these examples—these paradigms—for the graphic designer? Suppose you are presented with the following problems in search of a solution: You have a product made up of a dozen like-sized items, all rectangular in shape. How do you package them? You may look at an office building and see a structure four stories tall with three suites per floor. Could your package design follow that same sort of arrangement to contain the individual pieces? Likewise, you may come across a shoe rack made up of cubby holes, three holes across and four rows tall. Perhaps your items could be arranged this way, designed to slide in and out of the separate compartments. If the objects weren't rectangular, you might package them around an axis, like slices of pizza or spokes on a bicycle wheel.

Paradigms for packaging solutions are all around us. Your local Wal-Mart, the Great Pyramids of Giza, a Native American teepee, The Tower of Pisa—all architectural examples of the four basic forms in package design. The same forms in nature might be represented by a block of silica, an apophyllite crystal, a conifer tree, and a section of bamboo.

figure |2-20|

The four common packaging forms have correlations in nature, and are represented here in salt crystals, fossilized coral, apopyllite, and conus spurius (Alphabet Cone) seashells.

> *"The truly great designers arrived at their conclusions through the observation of nature: their masterpieces show close kinship of forms and design with plants or animals which have a similar problem to overcome."*
>
> **Paul Jacques Grillo,**
> **"Form, Function and Design"**

figure |2-21|

From nature, we recognize the Onion Layer paradigm, where each layer of an onion can be peeled away to reveal a smaller version of the onion inside. Structural applications of the paradigm include these Russian nesting dolls and a set of plastic storage bowls.

| SURVEY |

With globalization, more products and services will be introduced to a wider audience . . .

In five years, will you be doing more "brand" design?

Yes - I plan to increase my
brand design services.   78%

No - I don't plan to increase
my brand design services.   18%

No - I have little or no interest
in branding.   7%

Totals shown may be more or less than 100% due to rounding.

SOURCE: The International Council of Graphic Design Associations

| TIPS |

Paper and Bristol board should always be scored before folding to ensure straight, clean lines. This will also prevent surface graphics from "crackling" and becoming unsightly.

Scoring tools can be purchased at graphic arts, paper, and stationery and craft stores, ranging in price from around $3 to $30. In a pinch, though, I've had great success scoring paperboard by pressing firmly with an old, out-of-ink ballpoint pen. The roller ball glides smoothly over the surface, it feels comfortable in the hand, and the line width of the score is perfect for light to medium paper stock.

The Six-sided Box

Geometric forms made up of flat surfaces are known as polyhedrons. The prefix *poly* comes from the Greek, meaning "many," and *hedron,* meaning "planes" or "sides." The six-sided box is far and away the most common polyhedron used in storage structures. It can trace its lineage to wooden crates dating back to ancient Egypt, through the handmade display boxes of the eighteenth and nineteenth centuries and finally to the folding cardboard boxes of Robert Gair. Simple to construct and practical to stack, transport, and display, the six-sided box has become the most recognizable form in retail packaging. The basic cube, which we'll discuss here, can be altered, of course, with innumerable variations in its panel measurements, and methods for opening and closing the package are many, but the concept remains the same.

Working on the premise of creating an equal-sided cube, where each of the six sides is a square, first determine the overall measurement of each panel. It can be constructed as small as an inch per side, as might be used in individual packaging of confections or other small items, to several feet, as may be found on a package for large appliances such as televisions or washing machines. For our purposes here, a measurement of 2½ inches per side will fit on a standard sheet of 8½" x 11" paper. Sketch, first in pencil, a cube shown in perspective. This will help to visualize the structure. Imagine how this box will feel in your hands; at this point, don't consider the surface graphics of the box, but focus entirely on the physical structure. This is a good time to plan how the box will open and on which side. What do you consider to be the bottom of the cube? Will this side open as well, or will it be permanently sealed? These are all concerns of the package designer. Make some early decisions as to where the panels will be connected to one another. There are several ways in which the panels might connect (Figure 2-22), and each has its own advantage. If you were to cut out any of the patterns here and score and fold them at the dotted lines, you would be able to form them into cubes. However, a shape made this way will be difficult to construct. Edges where the figure should join don't have enough surface area to glue firmly, and the form won't have much structural integrity. Once you have an idea where edges should meet on your form, you will have to devise glue flaps—additional sections of the pattern that will serve as surfaces to hold glue and give your form stability (Figure 2-22).

Using one of the patterns in Figure 2-22, enlarge it to fit your sheet of paper. Then affix your drawing to a sheet of Bristol board, using the rubber cement technique you have learned. With an X-Acto knife, cut the pattern along its outside edge. Score along fold lines with a scoring tool (see Figure 2-22). Fold the sides to form the flat pattern into a cube. Finally, apply glue or double-sided tape to the connecting tabs to complete the construction of the box. You have just created a 3-D package mock-up.

The Pyramid

A more complex polyhedron is the pyramid. The pyramid can be designed with three or more sides, and its base will change accordingly. For instance, a three-sided pyramid will have a three-sided base; a four-sided pyramid will have a four-sided base, and so on. As with the simple cube, there are several ways to construct the pyramid. Three different configurations for the pyramid form are shown in Figure 2-23. Every pyramid has triangular sides that meet at a point. Because all the sides join at this single apex, the pyramid is a very sturdy form, with its weight at the base, that does not tip easily.

Create another pencil sketch of a pyramid to acquaint yourself with shape. Again, choose a pattern and construct a pyramid as you did the cube. If you begin again with a base of 2½ inches, you should be able to form your pyramid from a standard sheet of paper.

| **TIPS** |

End and tuck flaps—additional flaps of paper or board that fold in around a package closure—will add strength and security to the packaging. They help support the product and keep edges from bulging or bowing. For even more holding power, end flaps can be designed to interlock, which can help keep package sides square and parallel.

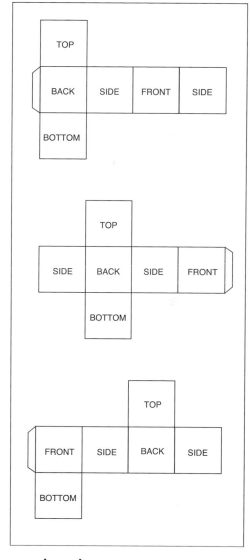

figure | **2-22** |

The six-sided box is one of the most common structures in packaging. Here are several different ways the panels can be aligned to create the cube.

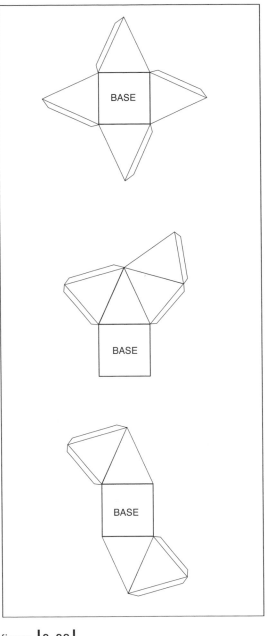

figure |2-23|

Three variations on the pyramid formed around a square base. Notice that each will have a different glue edge and opening.

The Cone

Polyhedra, as stated, are formed with flat planes as their sides. But it's also possible to create packages with curved sides. One such form is the cone. A cone is much like a pyramid in that its profile appears as a triangle, but the base is not three-, four-, or five-sided, but round, with a single, triangular side that turns around onto itself along the base. In packaging, the cone presents some special engineering problems. As you can see in Figure 2-24, a cone has only one straight edge for gluing. To secure the upright side to the base, the designer must incorporate a series of smaller tabs that fit along either the inside or the outside of the curve. Because of this, the cone is an uncommon form in package design, although not unheard of. In most cases,

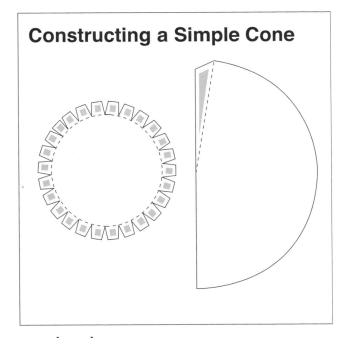

Constructing a Simple Cone

figure |2-24|

The cone—basically a pyramid with a round base—can be constructed this way. Note the numerous smaller glue tabs required to attach curved edges.

packagers use a crimped seal to join the side and base when designing with a cone.

Enlarge the pattern shown in Figure 2-24, as before, and create a cone with a flat base.

The Cylinder

The last basic shape for packaging is the cylinder. Like the cone, the cylinder has a single vertical side that curves around onto itself. Where the cone, however, has a single circular base, the cylinder has both a round base and top. The cylinder is a shape that is usually made from moldable materials such as plastic or metal, instead of paperboard, because of the same difficulties presented by the cone. But, like the cone, manufacturers have the ability to crimp the edges of paper together to join them. Notable examples include the cardboard packaging for food products such as ice cream or yogurt.

Variations on the basic cylinder include the truncated cone—a form with the top and bottom circles of different diameters.

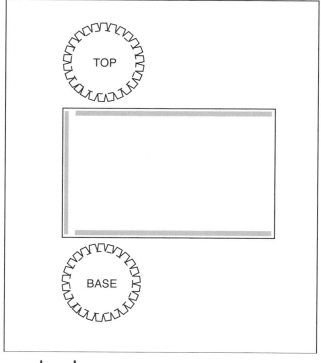

figure | 2-25 |

Standard 2-D patterns for making paperboard cylinders. Like the cone, small glue tabs make it possible to attach sides around the curves—in this case, both the top and bottom.

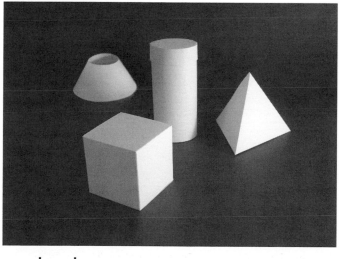

figure | 2-26 |

Three-dimensional models of the four basic forms described in this chapter.

COMMON MATERIALS

Four Common Packaging Materials and Their Attributes:

figure |2-27|

GLASS

Advantages

- Fairly inexpensive
- Air- and watertight
- Surface can be printed (screen printing) or labeled with paper or shrink-wrap labeling
- May be formed in standard or customized shapes
- Product is visible through the packaging

Disadvantages

- Fragile
- Heavy

METAL

Advantages

- Very strong
- Protects well against contamination
- Air- and watertight
- Surface can be printed (screen, litho, offset) or labeled
- Allows for high-speed filling, processing, and sealing

Disadvantages

- Package can dent easily
- Package can be difficult to open

figure |2-28|

figure |2-29|

PET

Advantages

- Very inexpensive
- Air and watertight
- May be formed in standard or customized shapes
- Lightweight
- Shatterproof
- Surface can be printed (screen, flexography) or labeled with paper or shrink-wrap plastic

Disadvantages

- Although PET can be formed easily, it cannot match the subtleties and complexities of glass
- Does not carry the same quality perception of glass

Cardboard/Paperboard

Advantages

- Very inexpensive
- Can be structured and folded to hold almost any object or shape
- Provides a total printing surface (litho, flexo, screen, gravure, offset, digital)
- Board is available in many thicknesses and finishes
- Recyclable

figure |2-30|

Disadvantages

- Package is not waterproof without expensive coating
- Cardboard does not carry the same quality perception as some other materials
- May not be as durable as other materials

PROFESSIONAL PROFILE

Mitch Lindgren

A founding member of Compass Design in Minneapolis, Minnesota, Mitch Lindgren serves as creative director, overseeing package design for high-profile clients such as Anchor Hocking, Dayton Hudson/Target Stores, General Mills, Land O'Lakes, and Pillsbury. He has a knack for bridging the creativity of his fellow designers and the marketing goals of his clients.

"Compass is a design firm that specializes in brand and package design," says Lindgren. "Our portfolio is made up of a wide variety of categories and clients, but the majority of our work is in food packaging."

Besides his love for packaging, Lindgren is also talented in hand-lettering, which brings another dimension to Compass's search for creative solutions to a package. "I have always had a love for type and solving design problems with type," he says. "I still produce designs using hand lettering and strong type elements. Packaging almost requires that the brand communication be a

© Compass Design

unique type approach, since it sometimes is the only graphic element on a package."

"My early influences were the type masters like [Herb] Lubalin and [Tom] Carnase. Later, it was designers like Neville Brody and Tim Girvin. These are very different approaches to type design, but you have to have a wide understanding of lettering approaches to solve a variety of packaging challenges. Each of these designers had an acute sense about legibility and lettering structure in order to push the envelope and still make the elements recognizable."

The Minneapolis area is home to a large assortment of industries, from Fortune 500 companies to small start-ups. As Lindgren sees it, this access to clients with local and national markets has fed the field beautifully. "It's helped the design community to grow and expand to be one of the strongest in the country," he says. "The array of design firms and design schools in the area make it a great place to start a career."

Throughout that career—over twenty five years—Lindgren has witnessed a few changes. "Design-wise," Mitch explains, "everything seems to be improving. What I mean is, there is a lot of good design on store shelves today, and that was not true ten years ago. Almost everyone has come to understand the need for a powerful package, and has improved their brand to better compete."

Despite this greater awareness in brand identity and design, Lindgren still finds that certain skills are not being attended to. "The challenge that I run into now is finding qualified talent that knows how to draw. Our firm requires strong conceptual designs in the early phases of a project. Pencil concepts achieve that more quickly. The drawing skills have slowly—and sadly—disappeared from a lot of design students.

"I will always look at a package as a designer first and a consumer second. The consumer in me gets frustrated at not being able to clearly see the difference between a Regular soft drink and its Diet counterpart. The designer in me sees a missed opportunity.

"The best part about package design is the variety of projects that you can work on. In the same week, we can be working on an ice cream, a pasta sauce, a tool line, and a new beer. You have to constantly watch what's going on in all categories of products. This means visiting a supermarket, a major discounter, big and small hardware stores, specialty gift shops, convenience stores, major department stores . . . and everywhere else that a consumer would buy a product."

Lindgren's advice for those new to the packaging field: "Don't get stuck in a style. It's way too early in your career to be designing and solving problems with the same approach and look. If, over time, you find a style that works for a lot of different brands and you find lots of clients that want it, then pursue it. But until you've listened to the demands of hundreds of different clients and their needs, you have to approach each project with an open mind and be willing to try new things. If a creative director asks to see something else or for you to try a different approach, do it. You will be surprised to find that you haven't come up with your best idea yet."

You can visit Compass Design on the Internet at www.compassdesigninc.com. ■

Giorgio Davanzo Design

figure | 2-31 |

The basic forms in use: the cube.

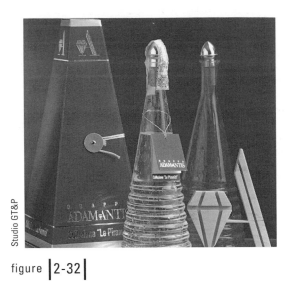

Studio GT&P

figure | 2-32 |

The pyramid.

Burt's Bees

figure | 2-33 |

The cylinder.

© Chuck Groth Graphic Design

figure | 2-34 |

The cone.

1. What are the major concerns every package must address?

2. In what ways is the packaging material determined by the product it contains?

3. What is meant by the phrase "form follows function"? How does that pertain to packaging?

4. What are the four basic forms used in packaging?

exercises

1. Consider each of the four packaging forms described in this chapter, find at least one other way to produce them that differs from the patterns presented, and produce a mock-up of it.

2. Find examples in your home or studio for each of the four forms. Make a list of the products they hold and the material used for the package. Do certain shapes and/or materials have distinct advantages for specific products?

3. Several design paradigms were described for the packaging forms in this chapter. Make a list of other paradigms for each form. How can they be applied to packaging?

CHAPTER

"Recognizing the need is the primary condition for design."

Charles Eames

Chapter Objectives

Consider the natural flow and hierarchy of packaging

Map a package's information across its surfaces

Introduce Gestalt psychology in visual perception

Explore the structural concerns of three-dimensional design

Introduction

Think of the last Olympics you saw on television. Many of the events went by so quickly, it wasn't until the replay that you were able to truly appreciate the individual efforts of the athletes. If the fifty-meter dash is over in five seconds or less, how much time are you able to devote to your favorite runner? To the other eight or more in the race? Package design can be seen in much the same way. As consumers move their carts through the aisles of a supermarket, they see many different packages each second. Familiar brands stand out because of recognizable typography, color, and shape. Others may strike interest because of their difference—they may not follow the standard size, shape, or even packaging material of the rest of the crowd in a particular product market.

figure |3-1|

An Olympic sprint is over in a flash.

figure |3-2|

We've all heard the aphorism "don't judge a book by its cover." Designers know that, on both practical and subconscious levels, nothing could be further from the truth.

The package designer knows that each piece has only a fraction of a second to reach out and communicate a myriad of information to its audience. Understanding how we perceive and interpret that information makes package design effective.

Every Package Tells a Story

Much like a movie or novel, every package has a story to tell. And each story moves along at its natural, determined pace. As a designer, you must have an understanding of that pace—the manner in which your audience will hold the package, scan across its surfaces, and interpret the information sensibly. Try it yourself—walking through the aisle of your favorite store, analyze a package you're drawn to and your response to it. What caught your attention? Was it the name of the product, a familiar brand, the color, the typography, the size, shape, or material of the packaging?

figure |3-3|

Well-designed book jackets are alluring and informative, letting the reader know just what kind of story awaits them inside. Expensive printing and quality graphics are also an indication of the faith the publisher has in the work. Like books, each package is a miniature bit of storytelling, with a beginning, middle, and end.

Initially, you are probably attracted to the package's front panel. This is usually your first introduction to the package, and it's a critical moment in the success or failure of the package. The saying goes, "you never get a second chance to make a first impression," and in the instance of packaging, the power of that maxim is particularly true. Studies have shown that a consumer views tens of thousands of different products during an average trip to the store—each package on the shelf gaining well under a second of attention before the buyer moves on or settles on a choice. The successful package grabs interest, setting it apart from the competitors stacked beside it, and speaks to its target, makes a connection, seals the deal. The front panel serves to identify the product, announce the brand or manufacturer, convey the "attitude" or personality of the contents, and differentiate it from its competition.

Once a package has enticed you to pick it up from the shelf, the next thing you will probably do is turn to the back panel of the package. This space is commonly used to reiterate the contents and describe the product's attributes in more detail. Special features unique to the product, simple instructions, or suggestions for use are usually displayed here. For a food package, this might include short recipes or serving suggestions, and extolments on its ingredients; a package for an electronic device may utilize this back panel to list technical information or point out ease of use. In any case, the back is the second most powerful panel of a package, allowing for a longer read, a chance to linger a little. The front fights for our interest, while the back reassures us that our choice was a sound one.

But what about the other panels of the package? Each has a part to play in the communication between manufacturer and consumer. Ingredients or contents, weights and measures, production information, toll-free numbers and Web addresses, warnings, guarantees, and Universal Pricing Codes all find their way onto modern packaging, and it's the designer's job to determine where they are placed. By establishing a coherent hierarchy of elements, the task can be accomplished in a manner that makes sense to the designer, manufacturer, and consumer.

Make a list of *all* the separate elements to be included on your package. Each line of text, every photo, illustration, or logo—everything your package needs to communicate—should be listed. Next, examine the list to find natural groupings—elements that logically go together. For example, phone numbers, addresses, and URLs might form a reasonable grouping. Reading through the list again, rank each element in order of its importance. In this way, you can determine the hierarchy for the information. To illustrate, the hierarchical list for elements on a box of muffin mix might read like this:

1. Product name

2. Company name

3. Logo (each panel)

4. Photograph

5. Slogan

6. Basic preparation instructions

PROFILES

Randy Mosher

© Randy Mosher Design

"I view packaging as an opportunity to tell a story," says designer Randy Mosher. "People are looking to the packaging to give them some idea of how they should think about the product." Mosher, owner of Randy Mosher Design in Chicago, takes that intimate feeling of storytelling and applies it to specialty and niche package design. His one-person firm produces packaging and marketing projects for craft breweries and a mix of other consumer-goods packaging and branding/identity work.

After starting right out of college at a large international packaging and identity firm—where he eventually became a creative director—Mosher found that he wanted other challenges. Fate provided the impetus to meld several interests: "When the first Gulf War tanked the agency I was working for, I found myself freelancing. I was a pretty avid home-brewer, so I knew a number of fellow brewers who were starting up small commercial breweries. Their need for packaging coincided with my interest in the historical aspects of graphics and package design, and so a new career direction was started."

What are the factors that weigh in when designing for specialty markets? "Efficacy, heritage, status, hipness, flavor, seductiveness, and many more aspects are important to people," according to Mosher, "and, of course, the mix changes dramatically from category to category. Usually there is an established framework for each product category,

7. Preparation diagram

8. Additional recipes

9. Nutrition facts

10. Net weight (ounces/grams)

11. Ingredients

12. Company mailing address/phone number/Web site address

13. UPC barcode

14. Paperboard recycling symbol

15. Carton-opening instructions

and sometimes these are quite ancient and even al-most ritualized. It's a challenge for a designer to break through and create a unique personality within the category language. If you go too far, you frighten people. They usually want evolution, not revolution, in the products they are drawn to."

What has worked for me to develop a voice as a designer is to put all the influences in a big tub and shake everything out, and see what happens to fit the problem of the moment.

© Randy Mosher Design

"I attended a very Bauhaus-influenced design pro-gram (University of Cincinnati), but I can't honestly say I ever had any kind of affinity for Helvetica, or, for that matter, what they were trying to teach me. I had always been interested in historical aspects of typography and design, a connection I'm pretty sure began with a childhood stamp collection. I have a large collection of antique typography and other ephemera, and if you look at some of that old work it's at an unbelievable level of skill. I find the past to be quite inspiring."

Although many of his designs bring to mind the lively hand-lettering and rich wood-cut quality of antique labeling, Mosher appreciates the current

toolbox for artists working today. "The digital revolution has altered the field almost beyond recognition in many ways," he says. "Computer technology is incredibly empowering. I could never offer my clients the product I do if I had to operate the way things were when I started out—mechanical keylines, presstype and all that cave-man technology. Of course, having a working knowledge of Adobe Illustrator does not make one a designer."

You can visit Randy Mosher Design on the Internet at www.randymosherdesign.com. ■

By ranking each element in this way, it becomes clearer how to orga-nize the information. Each panel of the package can then be "mapped." Since we know the front panel must convey the product and entice the consumer at first glance, it should probably include the first five ele-ments on the prioritized list. The back panel would be an appropriate place for elements 6 through 8, because they require more time to read and understand, and need to be easy to find. "Nutrition facts" might be placed on the left side panel, ingredients and addresses on the right side panel. The barcode and recycling symbol can be located on the

|TIPS|

When mapping a package, remember that the audience will generally follow this sequence when viewing—front, back, left side, right side, bottom. Informa-tion should be placed according to that order.

"The package design needs to reveal itself on all its sides and not just its 'face.' I encourage students to consider the package skin and to wrap the form with their designs and not just think of flat unrelated facets."

Judy Thompson,
St. Louis Community College

bottom of the box, because, while these elements are necessary for retail inventory and post-sale information, they are generally unimportant to the consumer. You may choose the top to display company logo, product name, and/or an image.

Almost everyone's pattern of moving across a package's surfaces follows this sequence: front (or front and top together), back, left side, right side, and bottom. If you understand this model and you have determined a hierarchy of the elements that will appear on a package, you can control the information and present it exactly in the order you envision and with the emphasis that suits your need.

Design by Jai Hoyer/
Photo by Tadashi Isozaki

figure │3-4│

This design utilizes its different surfaces and materials to make its statement. Container and package interplay to attract attention to these paper brads.

© Design by Jessica McEntire / Photo by
Tadashi Isozaki

figure │3-5│

The idea of "moving" across the various surfaces leads to this packaging piece. *Mind, body, and soul* all come together in this interconnected environment.

figure │3-6│

A typical *mapping* of box panels, following a written hierarchy. This kind of mapping allows the designer to organize information and control the flow and pace of the package text and imagery.

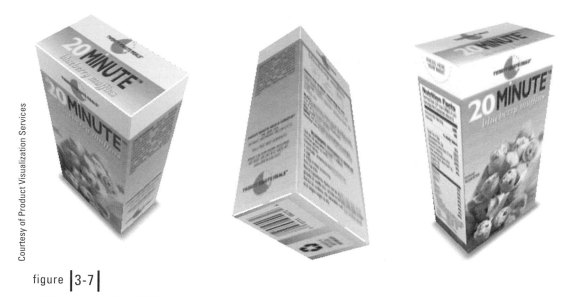

figure |3-7|

It's typical that our audience will see at least three sides of a three-dimensional package, from various angles, as shown in this series of photographs. The conscientious designer will work to engage these separate surfaces to keep the consumer involved in the design and progressing through the package's information.

Controlling the Flow: The Gestalt of 3-D Design

We've already discussed the conventional order in which the various panels of a package are experienced. But there are ways that designers can either reinforce this order or alter it toward a different sequence. When we view a three-dimensional object, such as a package, it is typical that we will see, at any given angle, three separate surfaces of the package at one time.

In the early part of the twentieth century, a group of psychologists led by Max Wertheimer developed a school of thought known as Gestalt. The theory of Gestalt was born in Germany in 1910. While traveling by train, Wertheimer—a thirty-year-old Czech-born psychologist—began to develop the idea when he saw flashing lights at a railroad crossing that reminded him of lights around a theater marquee. Why, he wondered, should the image of one thing (the train crossing) create such a strong connotation to something else so very different (such as a marquee)? Wertheimer began to explore other ways the mind interprets visual information and eventually teamed with two like-minded colleagues—Kurt Koffka and Wolfgang Kohler—to form a school of psychology called *Psychologische Forschung* (Psychological Investigation) and founded the theory of Gestalt principles that we relate now to design. The main thrust of this theory was that the human mind perceives a series of objects or

| TIPS |

Images that wrap around a corner of a package will draw the attention from one side to the other, as described in the Gestalt principle of continuation. Generally, though, it's a bad idea to use text to do the same: we tend to interpret the individual panels of a package as "pages," and small type that wraps around panels is often difficult to read.

PROFILES

Claudia Moran

© Obata Design

Claudia Moran is a senior partner of Obata Design, a St. Louis–based design consulting firm. She works primarily as a package designer for such national clients as Sara Lee Bakery Group, Energizer, Spectrum Brands, and Clorox.

Getting Started

"Our firm had hired a group of package designers when one of our large corporate clients (Anheuser-Busch) was eliminating their art department in the 1950s, so we have had a long history of package design at Obata Design. As a young artist, I was not that interested in type layout, i.e. the management of a large body of text. It is most certainly the foundation of annual report design, which is the other strength of our firm. But I liked the focus and conciseness of package design, plus the stimulation of the retail market and I found my niche there."

Evaluating a Package

"I think of each new packaging project as a poster. What designer is not tantalized by a poster? We have one canvas to attract the viewer and explain ourselves. With a package, we have such a short time to attract the consumer. The package has to scream off the shelf yet fit within its family appropriately to the product. There are often very tight constraints on printing as well, depending on the structure. Package impressions can run into the millions—and are often printed on flexo presses which would make an annual report designer cringe. I find these limitations stimulating and love to push the envelope. Flexo has come a long way over the course of my career and it continues to be fine-tuned.

"To evaluate a piece of packaging it has to be viewed in the marketplace—in context. Lovely as it may be on your client's credenza, it may completely disappear on the shelf among its competitors. Does it deliver on its promise? Is the package appropriate to the product category? Does it support the message of the brand and communicate the benefits in a clear and easily understood manner? Do the colors 'fit' the product? Or perhaps it is the tension created when the color or design does not 'fit' the category that draws the consumer's eye to your design. Getting the consumer to pick up your package is what should drive your effort.

"We look at each package assignment in phases. These are things to consider in the initial phase: the market audit, the consumer profile, the price, the tone or personality of the brand, the equities—especially if it is a redesign of an existing package. This initial phase, which we call Discovery, includes all of the information and data that we get from the client plus everything we can discover about the product in the marketplace. We survey similar product categories, check out competitors and assemble a creative brief that is blessed by the client. We meet with the design team and review the brief and the research. This is the fun part—the base of the design pyramid. We often offer ten or more initial concepts at this Design phase in order to stimulate conversation with the client. We are fairly informal, but we generally have two or three internal meetings to review concepts before the initial presentation. These meetings are set up to discuss each designer's rationale, to get feedback and to focus the effort on two or three conceptual directions. They help to inform those of us who are presenting to the client in order to direct the presentation and help the client to understand our motivation.

"Armed with client feedback (which may simply be one meeting or, more often, a series of meetings and revisions) we move into the Development phase where we flesh out one concept. We may continue to explore color and type variations while we pin down all the mandatory information, back and side panels, codes etc. If there are line extensions, we define them in this phase and nail down the method of differentiation, whether it is a ribbon or color change or some other device. We standardize the architecture of the main panel so that the consumer's eye sees the priority of the information, e.g., first brand, then product, then variety. Final art is produced with care. We work with the

© Obata Design

separator and printer to achieve what the client expects in a proof and then supervise the printing."

Advice to Students

"Do pencils—even if they are in pen. In other words, don't let a bad design go too far on the computer. The concept is most important. We can get so distracted by layer effects in PhotoShop, for instance, that we don't recognize that the concept wasn't on target in the first place. Nail down the design first."

Obata Design, Inc.

"Founded on a houseboat on the Mississippi in 1948, we have been a traditional design studio of about 25 employees, including 15 creatives, for over 50 years. Our focus is on serious business with many long-standing relationships with clients of 10 years or more. Our strengths include annual reports, corporate communications, package design and web development, although our experience runs the gamut of design."

You can visit Obata Design on the Web at www.obatadesign.com. ■

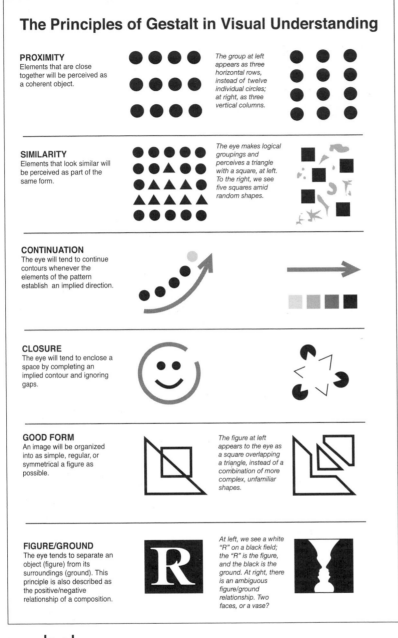

The Principles of Gestalt in Visual Understanding

PROXIMITY
Elements that are close together will be perceived as a coherent object.

The group at left appears as three horizontal rows, instead of twelve individual circles; at right, as three vertical columns.

SIMILARITY
Elements that look similar will be perceived as part of the same form.

The eye makes logical groupings and perceives a triangle with a square, at left. To the right, we see five squares amid random shapes.

CONTINUATION
The eye will tend to continue contours whenever the elements of the pattern establish an implied direction.

CLOSURE
The eye will tend to enclose a space by completing an implied contour and ignoring gaps.

GOOD FORM
An image will be organized into as simple, regular, or symmetrical a figure as possible.

The figure at left appears to the eye as a square overlapping a triangle, instead of a combination of more complex, unfamiliar shapes.

FIGURE/GROUND
The eye tends to separate an object (figure) from its surroundings (ground). This principle is also described as the positive/negative relationship of a composition.

At left, we see a white "R" on a black field; the "R" is the figure, and the black is the ground. At right, there is an ambiguous figure/ground relationship. Two faces, or a vase?

figure |3-8|

The Gestalt psychological principles, as they pertain to visual interpretation. The seven principles are illustrated here, and when understood and applied by a designer, they can carry the concept or imagery of a design further and with deeper meaning and impact than just its color palette, typography, and images.

shapes and that, by relating them through proximity, similarity, continuation, closure, form, and figure/ground, interprets them as a unified whole. That is, the way the human brain is wired, we *look at* a series of elements, but we *see* an overall grouping.

By employing the principles of Gestalt in package design, it is possible to direct a viewer along the package's surfaces in the precise order desired. Similar shapes or colors create a sense of unity, implied direction leads the eye in very predictable patterns—even the amount of space between elements affects the pace and flow of their perception. If it is your intention to direct your audience, not from front panel to back panel, as is natural, but rather from the front to the right side panel, this can be accomplished by using the Gestalt principles of continuation or similarity to draw the eye from one plane to the next. Remember that the principle of continuation tells us that any implied contour or direction will lead the viewer in the same direction. Lines, shapes, colors, or even typography that extends from one panel to the next will certainly take us across these planes. The same can be said for similar shapes or colors; since we are able to view more than one surface of most 3-D packaging, any element that draws us from one point to another can direct the "flow" of information.

Psychologically, humans are always searching for these visual connections, and since we can usually see more than one side of a three-dimensional object at any one time, designers need to be cognizant of the interplay those sides will have in the overall perception of a package. For this reason, most package designers prefer to explore their design concepts on paper with pencil or

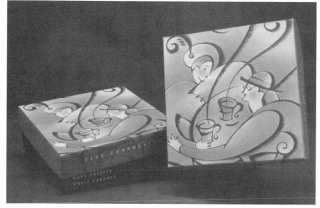

© Hornall Anderson

figure |3-9|

By letting the illustration flow across corners, the designer has prompted interaction between the package sides.

© Crayon Design

figure |3-10|

Every surface is addressed in the design of this sushi set tin.

© Crayon Design

figure |3-11|

A retro-styled martini set features full "design-in-the-round."

figure |3-12|

These beverage packages use the principles of Gestalt psychology to direct the viewer's eye and organize information.

figure |3-13|

By wrapping images and colors around panels, the designer has created a greater sense of depth and interaction between the package sides.

pen, quickly sketching out broad ideas, roughing in imagery and text to immediately see how the panels will interact when viewed together. It's also what makes package design a particularly challenging and complex discipline in the graphics field.

"The design process begins on paper. Quick, rough sketches are a good way to evaluate ideas. Once a number of strong concepts have been developed, work can move to the computer."

Daryl Woods, owner of *Public Image Design*

The Importance of the Thumbnail

A common mistake is the failure to apply the effort, attention, and dedication to this sketching phase. At this point, anything is possible, which can be a daunting prospect; with any number of possible solutions, how to choose? Many designers have been stymied by so much freedom. In the field of novelists, it's often described as "writer's block"—so many possibilities leading to indecision and finally, a sort of creative paralysis, leaving the writer staring blankly at the keyboard. Designers can avoid the trap by maintaining a respect for the sketching—or "thumbnail"—stage of visual problem solving. Draw quickly and generally as many different ideas as you can. Rearrange elements, play with their scale or proximity to each other, change color palettes, push the envelope. These thumbnails do not have to be, and in fact should not be, formal, finished drawings. Instead, develop concepts, focusing more on the "feel" of the arrangements, the overall composition. Broad shapes serve you better here than detailed images. Remember: the package will often have to communicate its message from a distance with general lines, colors, and contours.

This is the time to play. Don't be afraid to explore any idea and investigate any avenue that comes to mind. Try various shapes or orientations for the package. It's not unusual to produce upwards of fifty to a hundred thumbnails for a given project.

The Development of a Typical Package

When you see a particularly successful package on a store shelf, it's easy to forget the many steps and metamorphoses the package went through before it was ready to market. People are often unaware of the involved process of design development. With so much riding on the execution—from money spent on graphic design, research, production, and marketing to the public's perception and acceptance of the package—designers and manufacturers alike follow rigorous creative and evaluative procedures to produce the most effective solutions to the problems inherent in design development. Below are some of the stages a typical package goes through from concept to production:

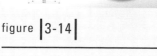

figure |3-14|

Every detail is worked through before sending a package to production. In this case, computer-aided modeling was used to explore a bottle's form.

1. **A product is created.** This may be as simple as making the decision to market salt or as involved as designing and manufacturing a personal computer, but in almost every case, the product decision comes before the packaging decision.

2. **Client and designer meet to discuss the project.** Many times, a client will know exactly what makes a terrific product, but has no clue what makes a creative and communicative package. These first meetings allow for an exchange of ideas, a chance for each side of the table to ask questions, and helps to focus designer and client on the product's place in the market, the "attitude" the client wants to project with the packaging, and the overall goals both client and designer hope to achieve on the project.

3. **Designer writes a design brief.** Designer will research the product as well as the existing market competition. A written brief, reflecting that research, market analysis, competition strengths and weaknesses, and an overall vision for the package design process, is presented to the client. Thorough briefs may include summaries of the client/designer meetings, demographic and social profiles of the perceived audience or market of the product, photographs of similar products already in the marketplace, analyses of competitive packages evaluating their structures, styles, practicality, color palettes, typography, and market effectiveness, as well as a formal statement of the goals of the new package design (the target audience the client/designer hopes to address, projected costs, messages to be conveyed, etc.). The more detailed the brief, the more the client and designer will understand the expectations of the package's focus and how to achieve them.

4. **Rough concepts are created.** Designer and art director work to visually brainstorm—many concepts are explored through thumbnail sketches and promising ideas are developed into tighter roughs. The best several concepts are presented to the client for feedback. Different clients have different expectations, but it is not unusual to present anywhere from four to ten concepts.

5. **Feedback is assimilated into tighter composites and mock-ups.** After hearing client critiques of the presentation, one to four ideas are usually picked to develop to the next stage. Concerns of both client and designer are addressed and several ideas are carried to the level of tight composites, or "comps."' Full-size mock-ups are produced to determine how the design concepts work in 3-D. Structural concerns of the package are often worked through at this point. Mock-ups are usually presented to the client for approval.

6. **Focus group research is conducted.** Since a package must appeal to the public and not just the client or artist, many firms will employ focus groups to determine not only how functional the market will find the packaging, but also how communicative it is. Group participants' reactions to all aspects of the package are recorded, from the clarity of its message to the emotional responses conjured by its colors, typography, imagery, and structure. Focus groups are often formed considering multiple demographic populations, some conducted as informal roundtables (qualitative), and others as more structured with individual questionnaires (quantitative). Variations of the package are tested and compared with those of competitors. Obviously, the importance of this qualitative and quantitative research increases with the size of the target audience; it's more crucial to reach a wide audience with a product like laundry detergent than with a niche item such as home décor.

7. **Concepts are firmed up.** With the reactions of client, designer, and focus groups as a guide, some concepts can be rejected and others pursued. Designs can be adjusted, taking into account all the reactions and feedback received. Sometimes these are presented directly to the client; other times, additional focus groups are assembled to monitor progress. At this stage, the design is close to its final form. Mock-ups are created and the last kinks are worked out.

8. **Package design is finalized.** With client approval of the design, text is copy-proofed for errors and content, and final artwork—photography or illustration—is completed by in-house or freelance artists and incorporated into the package design. The design is applied to the digital template and all files are prepared for production. Digital files must be flawless; every font used must be included for production, every image file must be in the proper format for your service bureau in CMYK, and all measurements must be accurate. If a designer leaves any room for error in the production files, he or she may expect errors as the piece is produced. Detailed and accurate printer flats should be provided along with your electronic files for the service bureau to follow.

9. **Press checks and final proofreading are done.** More often than not, the designer (and sometimes the art director, creative director, and product manager) will go on-site to witness the package being printed and produced. The reason for this is to ensure quality control by verifying that specifications are followed, proper paper stock is used, colors match those intended, folds occur where they are supposed to, and to monitor the general process. Press checks are the very last chance to catch any errors that may have slipped through the proofreading and design processes before many thousands of the package are printed.

10. **Product is packaged, sorted, and shipped for distribution.** This is the last stage of production before the package ends up in the hands of the consumer. Packages are filled and shipped, and the truest test of their creativity, structural integrity, and production quality comes as they enter the marketplace.

As you continue, you'll find certain themes or arrangements that seem to work better than others. Identify the strongest of these and begin to refine them further, though still keeping things loose. The only criteria here should be that your ideas begin to communicate what's necessary. As long as your concepts are appropriate and relevant, they deserve exploration at this point.

Eventually, a design is honed to several developed concepts. Only then should you bring your ideas to the computer and begin to make some more formal decisions such as type choices, photographic images, and their placement. Often, the urge to work on-screen is so strong that an artist will be lured to begin their digital design too early.

The problem is that computer-generated typography and images have a certain "finished" quality that's inherent to the medium. Type is straight, photographs clear, colors bright. Not to overstate it, but these impressions can serve as a trap; a concept may be chosen before it has been fully explored or developed. Package designer Claudia Moran, of Obata Design in St. Louis, puts it this way: "Don't let a bad design go too far on the computer." Moran continues, " . . . the concept is most important. We can get so distracted by layer effects in Photo-Shop, for instance, that we don't recognize that the concept wasn't on target in the first place. Nail down the design first."

Interestingly, many clients are becoming aware of this phenomenon and have been insisting on seeing only hand-rendered roughs during the developmental stages of a package so that they can focus on the strength of the idea and not be wooed too early by the flash of digital graphics. Once the design is brought to screen, however, the graphic artist has a wealth of tools on hand. Typefaces should be chosen carefully, with attention to their legibility, the "attitude" of the font, and any connotations that may be associated with them. Imported imagery should be of a sufficient resolution to reproduce well (in most professional packaging, the print processes require the artwork to be at least 300 dpi at actual—or run—size).

Applying Your Design to the Template

It's usually necessary to create a digital template for the desired package, using precise measurements for the panels. Once this template is established, the design can be

| TIPS |

Thumbnail sketches are best executed by working very broadly at first. Early thumbnails may simplify elements into basic shapes to understand the compositional relationships before refining them with actual text or images.

figure |3-15|

When brainstorming ideas, create as many quick thumbnail sketches as you can. But don't spend too much time on each—the goal is to explore broad concepts and general compositions. Promising ideas can later be developed further.

| SURVEY |

"Inspiration" helps to foster creativity and innovation. Creative professionals can find "inspiration" in many ways: through people and cultures; by observing and experiencing nature; and in objects or engineered systems (such as music, politics, space travel, city living . . .).

What inspires you most?

People	**29%**
Nature	**43%**
Objects or engineered systems	**32%**

Totals shown may be more or less than 100% due to rounding.

SOURCE: The International Council of Graphic Design Associations

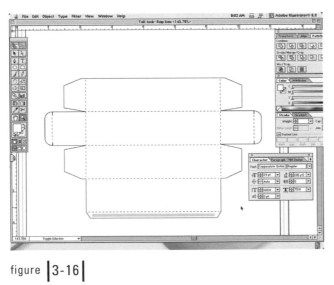

figure | 3-16 |

Creating a digital template.

refined further, modified to fit the exact dimensions of the package, and moved around the various surfaces easily. This is also the time to apply client or focus group feedback to the work. What suggestions or concerns could be addressed? Are there new ideas that should be examined before the package is finalized? *The evaluation process is critical to successful packaging.*

There are many different applications of computer software available to the package designer; Adobe Illustrator, Adobe Photoshop, Alias Studiotools, Rhinoceros, and 3DStudioMax are all common within the design and production community. But, whether you are using a software application in or out of the mainstream, it is always advisable to check with your printer/service bureau to be certain that your work will be compatible with their systems. Failure to do so is an invitation for trouble that can be easily avoided by checking beforehand. Often, it is just a matter of saving the work into a universal computer format for production, such as PDF, EPS, or TIF.

SUMMING IT UP

The physical nature of packaging is what sets it apart from other two-dimensional applications of design. A package's multiple surfaces call for a distinct division of information and elements. Like a story, the package panels allow for the product's "narrative" to unfold, with a beginning, middle, and end; understanding the natural pace and flow of a package permits the designer to tell that story in a compelling, interesting, and organized way.

Hierarchal organization of information, an understanding of Max Werthiemer's Gestalt principles of visual perception, thumbnail exploration, and digital execution of a design all lead to the creation of successful packaging mock-ups. Once these skills are mastered, the designer is limited only by imagination.

1. Take a cardboard box and disassemble it, being careful to keep it in one piece. Draw a diagram of the flat box and label the front, back, sides, top, and bottom. On each section of your diagram, note the type of information each panel contains. Do the same for another package and compare the diagrams. Are there similarities in the placement of information? Notable differences?

2. Find several existing packages. Using your understanding of the way consumers view multipaneled packages, list examples of Gestalt principles that were used by the designer. How effective are they in directing the flow of information?

3. Using one of the existing packages, carefully measure each panel. Create first a pencil sketch and then a digital template for the package. Print and try to assemble your own version of the box. Does it work? Are there any other ways to construct the package that might be simpler or more efficient?

CHAPTER

4

> *"Mockups are essential. You can't get an accurate idea of the way sides meet up or how type will look without them. Clients like to see mockups too, not only for evaluation, but also for promotion. Once I made an olive oil mockup for a client and she took it with her to conventions and when she went to see buyers. Because the oils were in Greece, she had nothing else to show."*
>
> **Diane Benjamin, Pomegranate Design**

Chapter Objectives

Understand the power of mock-ups in package design

Learn the elements of successful printer's flats

Introduction

Once a concept is strong and the design has been made to conform to the template, it's time to see how it will actually work as a three-dimensional package. This is done by creating a mock-up of the piece. Mock-ups are models of the package—cut, folded, and assembled just as the final printed work will be. They are usually produced at actual size, although a designer may choose to scale down early mock-ups to get a general "feel" of the package shape and panel interaction quickly, while fleshing out ideas.

Package designs are applied to a template, printed, affixed to Bristol paperboard for strength, cut, scored, and folded into shape. This way, the solution may be viewed from any angle, held in hand, or set up on a shelf alone or alongside competitors'

Design by Daniel Shinn

figure |4-1|

A flat printed design is assembled into a 3D prototype.

packaging to better see how effectively it's communicating. (Follow the steps in the preceding chapter for creating 3-D forms.) Working with Bristol board, early determinations can be made as to how rigid or flexible the substrate should be to contain and protect the product, how well the structure has been thought through, how clearly it communicates up close and from a distance, and the natural "flow" of its panels and elements.

The mock-up also serves as a very useful market research tool. Most products are tested and evaluated through extensive focus group studies to measure consumer perception of the design, and to determine ease of handling and practicality of the package structure in terms of product containment, protection, and communication. The full-size mock-up makes this kind of exploration possible.

THE PURPOSE OF THE MOCK-UP

Creating a mock-up of a package design concept may seem laborious, and a step best reserved for the final stages of the product's development. Nothing could be further from the truth. Once a designer becomes comfortable with the basic mock-up techniques, he or she won't consider them tedious—in fact, producing preliminary mock-ups will identify problems and concerns in the package design early on in the process, and be an invaluable tool as a package's voice develops.

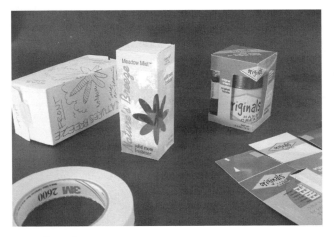

figure | 4-2 |

Sketch models and 3D prototypes allow the designer to envision the package concept in action.

An effective mock-up will display each of these qualities:

- True to scale of the actual package, even if not presented at full size

- Accurately depicts the typographic treatment and image application intended for the final package

- Gives as close an approximation as possible of all elements such as text, diagrams, and logos

- Depicts a reasonable placement of elements

- Serves as a communicative representative of the product, reflecting client goals and speaking to consumer needs

Types of Mock-ups

By the time a package has made it onto a shelf in the marketplace, it has usually gone through a rigorous system of research and testing. It's evaluated according to a wide range of goals, including package cost and material availability, protection and containment of the product, size, shape, color, and text, shipping practicality, communication clarity, shelf display scenarios, and consumer perception. If it fails in any of these areas, the package is unlikely to succeed in the market. The three-dimensional mock-up is an indispensable tool in this testing process.

Mock-ups can usually be divided into two categories: Sketch Models and 3-D Prototypes.

The Sketch Model is a very rough three-dimensional model of the package. Designers will often construct these Sketch Models quickly with Bristol board and tape. A Sketch Model may even be produced with blank panels to be drawn on with pencil or marker as the concept develops. Though still made to scale, these rough models serve as dimensional sketchpads—explorations and trials to organize elements and experiment with construction ideas. Unless the form and structure of a package is already determined (as may be the case in a DVD package or a mass-market cereal box, for example) a designer may develop several of these Sketch Models, trying out varying configurations and shapes. These models are generally used solely as design tools—allowing the designer to more accurately envision a package's structure and form—and are rarely shown to clients. In all instances, however, the Sketch Model is an important stepping-stone along the way toward a design.

3-D Prototype mock-ups differ from Sketch Models in both surface treatment and construction. After the mapping of elements, the Sketch Model explorations, and the package template creation, the design process leads toward the 3-D Prototype. A prototype is produced when a design is at a stage where it can be accurately applied to a template and presented as a faithful representation of the final package. In most cases, these prototypes involve computer-generated typography with photographic or digital images from which high-quality prints are made. To approximate the eventual thickness of the package, these prints are glued to Bristol board or another appropriate substrate and a very precise mock-up is made. A 3-D Prototype should stand as a true and convincing representation of the final package design, and care should be taken to make it appear and feel like the

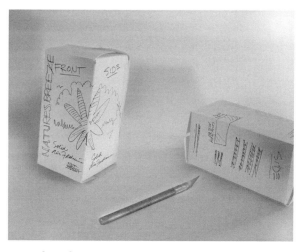

figure |4-3|

The Sketch Model allows the designer to better explore a packaging form early in the creative process.

| SURVEY |

Do you need excellent computer skills to be an excellent designer?

Yes, the best designers have
excellent computer skills   **26%**

No, but it helps to have
excellent computer skills   **44%**

No, you do not need excellent
computer skills to be an
excellent designer   **34%**

Totals shown may be more or less than 100% due to rounding.

SOURCE: The International Council of Graphic Design Associations

PROFILE

Ronald de Vlam

© Webb Scarlett de Vlam

Ronald de Vlam is President of Webb Scarlett de Vlam in Chicago, Illinois. In 1992 de Vlam teamed with partners Ian Webb and Felix Scarlett to form Webb Scarlett de Vlam in the heart of London. With forty-plus employees and additional offices in Sydney, Australia, and Chicago, Webb Scarlett de Vlam has positioned itself as a powerful force in product design, branding, and marketing. Providing services for clients such as Schweppes, Chivas Regal, Pepsi, and Cover Girl, de Vlam understands the creativity and objective analysis required to develop effective branding strategies, new-product development, and packaging graphics.

De Vlam describes the typical phases of a packaging project:

- Phase 1: "Design Exploration: The free flow of ideas initially generated as sketches which, with a second round of development and refinements, are presented to the client as color visuals and/or Sketch Models."

- Phase 2: "Concept Development: Three to four lead concepts will be evaluated with consumers to determine which comprehensives, appearance models, or working prototypes will be required. This is also a good phase to integrate production and operations for their input in potential "can/cannot do' scenarios."

- Phase 3: "Design Specification: From consumer and technical feedback, we begin to specify the range and SKU extensions of the brand. Copy, barcodes and nutritional information for each label will now be strictly applied to front and back labels for artwork specifications. CAD engineering files will bounce between our designers and the toolmaker and manufacturers of the packaging. Once the design is frozen, we instigate an official sign-off process for production."

- Phase 4: "Design production: Here our involvement is less intensive since we have handed our baton over to the production engineers. However, as first-off production samples run off the line, we can make critical interceptions, if necessary, to ensure the design has retained its intended design integrity."

"This process changes with each assignment," de Vlam says. "Some assignments require more consumer testing between and during the design phases. Other projects will fast-track and skip one, or sometimes even two, of the phases."

The role of a designer is to optimize the process and to get the best out of limited possibilities that prerequisite paradigms may put on an assignment.

De Vlam also shares some insights on the selection of packaging materials. "Sometimes," he says, "a material choice is not negotiable. For instance, glass is the industry standard for gins and whiskeys. PET is a second choice, but only for the less premium brands as consumers, rightly so, make a value perception between glass and plastics.

"Seldom do we suggest or specify a material and process not tried and tested within the category. This may sound defeatist; however, since most packaging is mass-produced and filled at 300+ per minute, there is little enthusiasm to counter this momentum with slower, heavier, or more costly proposals."

But that's not to say that a category material is entirely set in stone. "There is always room for innovation," de Vlam explains. "For instance, our design for Mistic RE (Cadbury Schweppes) was the first energy drink to be launched in an aluminum bottle. Our tubs for the Filippo Berio spreads were rotationally molded, a process that can produce a highly detailed embossed surface.

The packaging material and printing substrate are extremely important. The role of a designer is to optimize the process and to get the best out of limited possibilities that prerequisite paradigms may put on an assignment.

"Another key criteria that can drive material choice for a brand is its stance on environmental issues. The Aveda brand, for instance, will only use recycled materials for its packaging and ensure all its products and packaging are biodegradable or recyclable."

For those interested in the field of package design, de Vlam has these words: "Packaging is a fascinating design medium. I compare it to fashion design. It is very vibrant, exciting, and challenging. However, you will need to be up for the challenges. Many clients will make low-risk, commercially sound decisions, sometimes shelving a design for which you have bled your fingers the previous month. Sometimes, you will overestimate a consumer's acceptance of a design that you may love, but the consumer absolutely hates. You will need to be a team player, collaborating with other designers, sometimes from other agencies. But most of all, you will need to show that you understand the relationship between a consumer and a brand. Whichever discipline you are pursuing, if you want to exploit your energies in packaging design, make sure you know how to wear the consumer hat and the brand hat, consecutively."

You can visit Webb Scarlett de Vlam on the Internet at www.wsdv.com. ■

figure | 4-4 |

A Prototype mock-up provides a faithful representation of the finished package design.

Design by Jacob Day Steele /
Photo by Tadashi Isozaki

figure | 4-5 |

A mock-up, made before an actual piece goes into production, gives a direct demonstration to designer and client of how the package will be constructed and how well the design is working.

finished piece will. The 3-D Prototype is a powerful tool in the design presentation before a client, because it demonstrates a package's effectiveness in ways that a verbal description or two-dimensional image never could; the mock-up is as close to the actual package as either designer or client can get before the work goes into production, a hold-in-the-hand realization of purpose, intent, and vision.

The Roles of the Mock-up

Beyond looking good and showing that the design and structure are functional, what other purposes does the mock-up serve? To best understand, it's a good idea to consider the differing viewpoints from which the package will be judged.

A client has a concept for a product. In most cases, there are strong feelings about the goals for presenting it to the public. Target audiences are defined, issues of quality, value, and attitude are identified. A client may say, "I have a product that needs a package. I have to be sure that the package reflects my product and my company in a true manner, that it separates my product from the competition, that it protects it from production to sale, that it reaches out to the consumer."

A designer may look at the same assignment and say, "This package must protect the product, and thus it has to be structurally sound. Equally important, it must convey the client's message in a communicative, compelling manner. I want the package to be creative, enticing, and functional, all in a way that pleases the client."

The package's manufacturer will consider the project and think, "This package must be well-constructed and functional. I will need precise information on the package's intent and clear instructions for printing and assembly of the piece."

Finally, the consumer comes into the picture, and says, "When I'm shopping, I usually like to find what I want quickly and easily. I'm drawn to certain packages by their style and 'look'; the feeling I get from a package is important to me. I also want all the information I need without having to search for it. With all the choices on the shelf, I'm apt to pick a product that feels like a good fit for me, my personality, and my lifestyle."

Before a product goes into production, its mock-up is tested and evaluated to establish how well it answers all these goals and expectations. The designer studies the prototype to be certain the piece has met the creative goals set out in the design brief. The manufacturer uses the mock-up to determine the most appropriate board stock and printing methods required to produce the package, devising cost estimates and finish schedules. Consumer focus groups are assembled. The mock-up and product are presented to these groups, often consisting of between four to eight people, and their responses are recorded. Focus groups are asked to voice opinions along a wide array of pertinent topics, ranging from their perceptions of the product's quality, to the practicality of the package, to how the package makes them "feel." If we remember some of the research done by Louis Cheskin in the 1930s to 1950s, it becomes clear how important these focus groups are in the design's development. The slightest change in color, type choice, size, and placement of images can all radically influence a package's acceptance in the marketplace. Strengths and weaknesses are documented and, usually, adjustments are made. After all this, the client reviews the designer's solution, looks at the manufacturer's cost projections, listens to the focus groups' responses and examines his or her own feelings about the design, and determines if it meets the customer's needs or if further work must be done.

GETTING THE PACKAGE READY FOR PRODUCTION

When a package design is finalized, it must be readied for production. Once again, the work goes back to two-dimensional form and a production flat is created. A production flat is a flat representation of the package, with specific information and notations necessary for the production crew to print, fold, and assemble the package.

| TIPS |

Careful consideration must go into every color choice. Market research of competing brands can show not only common color schemes for a category, but also areas that will help a package stand out from the crowd.

Are certain color choices accepted or avoided? Why? For instance, if a designer chooses green as the dominant color for a coffee package to emphasize its "natural" or "organic" qualities, he or she should also be aware that in that category, green is almost universally recognized as the indicator for decaffeinated coffee.

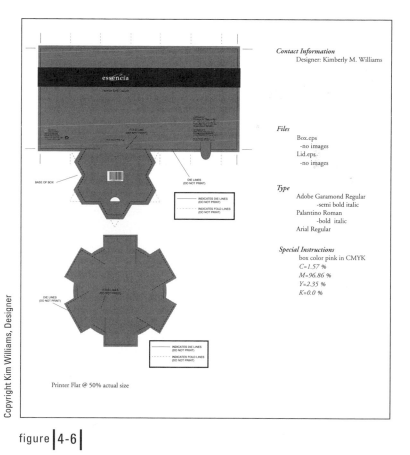

figure | 4-6 |

When submitting a design for mass production, it's common to provide a production flat along with the mock-up for those unfamiliar with the package to follow.

CHECKLIST FOR PRINTER INDICATIONS:

Information and indication marks for sending work out for production. These are the major issues to indicate, although special or unusual projects may require more specific indications.

Indicate Crop Marks
    Crop marks show the printer the exact dimensions the final piece will be trimmed to. They are indicated by this symbol:

    ¬|

Indicate Folds and Cuts
    The printer is alerted to folds in the final piece by this symbol:

    – – – –

    Cuts are indicated by this symbol:

    ————

Indicate Perforations
    Perforations are called out to the printer and production manager by this symbol:

    . . . . .

Register Marks
    Register marks are used to assure precise alignment of several layers in a piece, including color separations, special overlays, etc.
    Registers are indicated by this symbol:

Indicate any other special considerations
    Be sure to alert your printer to any special things to keep in mind, including custom die-cuts, unusual folds, 'bleeds,' or special processes.

LIST:

• Font file names used in the document
    (use the EXACT font name, such as 'ITC Franklin Gothic Demi')

• Each subfile name
    (scans, placed images, etc.)

• Document page size

• Number of pages

• Contact information
    (your name and how you can be reached, your company name, as well as any other person who should be contacted if there's a question, problem, missing file, etc. Include after-hours contact information, if applicable.)

figure | 4-7 |

A checklist and guide for common printer indications. Many service bureaus will provide such a checklist to help in proper file preparation.

One of the first steps in producton is to meet with a representative of the service bureau that will be doing the printing. Issues to clarify early on include digital platform and software support, image resolution requirements, bleed requirements, and color specifications. If the package has been designed on a Macintosh, will the service bureau be able to handle files in that platform? At the time of this writing, the Macintosh computer platform is the industry standard for most print shops, although many are expanding to dual platforms (Macintosh and PC) for better service. It's also important to find out if the software used to design the piece is compatible with the bureau's system and of congruent versions. Again, industry standards lean toward Macintosh-based software such as Adobe Illustrator, Adobe Photoshop, Adobe InDesign, and Quark Xpress, but many of these programs are available in both Mac and PC formats. Image resolution is another key issue to discuss. Scanned images should be, generally, at least 200–300 ppi (pixels per inch) for good reproduction. Images below that resolution will appear fuzzy and pixilated, but different printing processes will have different requirements. Most packaging will need to include a bleed area— the image/color area that extends slightly beyond the trimmed size of the package—so that the image goes all the way to the edge of the paperboard. Each commercial printer has a preference for how large this bleed area must be. Standard bleeds are produced between ⅛ and ¼ of an inch. Also, files should be produced in the appropriate color mode for final printing. If a file is produced in RGB (red-green-blue) but will be printed in CMYK (cyan-magenta-yellow-black), the designer can expect unwelcome color shifts when the piece is printed; the service bureau can usually convert the files to the proper mode, but at an added expense.

With this information in hand, the designer produces a production flat, which depicts the package in flat form as it will print on paper or board. All information the production crew will need to cut, fold, and assemble the work is indicated in clear and specific detail. The outline of the package shape is indicated with a solid black line, as are all lines to be cut. Scores and folds in the package are indicated with a dashed line. Perforations are noted by a dotted line, but it's never a bad idea to label these as "perforations" (or "perfs," for short), since there is the possibility of them being mistaken for the dashed-line folds. Any other special considerations specific to a particular package, such as custom die-cuts, unusual folds of unique printing processes—anything out of the ordinary that you feel should be noted—are indicated on the production flat to avoid costly confusion.

A complete production flat should also list each font (typeface) used in the package design by its exact name, such as *ITC Franklin Gothic Demi* as opposed to simply *Franklin Gothic*. This ensures that the proper font files are installed. Each subfile—every placed graphic (logos, barcodes) and every scanned image or photograph—must also be listed. Glue areas should be labeled as well. Finally, the designer supplies contact information, such as designer/project manager names, addresses, phone numbers where they can be reached, and e-mail addresses. This enables the production crew to clarify the problem or alert the designer or client if there is a question, problem, missing or corrupt file, or any other concern that may hold up production of the package.

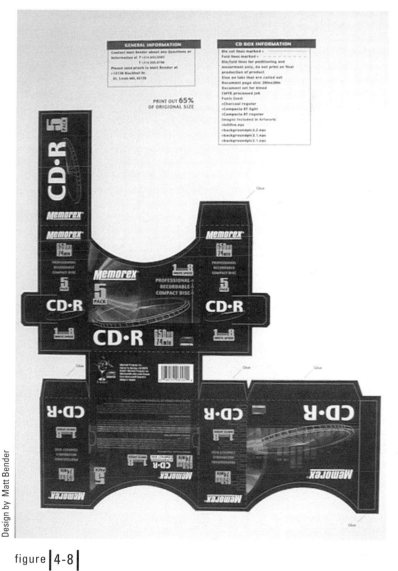

Design by Matt Bender

figure | 4-8 |

A complete production flat includes all the information required to accurately print, fold, and assemble the package.

Case Study

Designing a baking mix package and creating a full-size mock-up.

The Problem

To design a package for a mid-level baking mix (quick, easy-to-make blueberry muffins), using four-color printing on paperboard stock. Package should conform to typical baking goods products in size and structure, but reach out to an audience perceived as professional, "on-the-go," and slightly up-scale. Graphics should reflect quality, ease of use, clarity, and organization.

Hierarchy

The designer lists the required elements as determined by the client and establishes a hierarchy, ranking the elements in the order of importance. They decide that the front panel of the box should include the company logo, brand name, product name, net weight (American and metric), and an enticing photograph of the prepared product. They research competing products and evaluate them for effectiveness, graphic and structural treatments, and overall communication.

Initial Design

The designer creates a series of thumbnail sketches. Early concerns deal with the overall feel of the package, with the main focus on the design composition. Placement and scale of elements, color combinations, and flow of information are all explored. Many thumbnails are produced before a concept is chosen for further development.

Once the designer decides on a composition, they work out the finer details. Different typographic solutions and color schemes are investigated. The logo is created. Simple line drawings are created for mixing instructions. The package's "voice" begins to come through. At this point, various structures of the box are looked at, and a two-dimensional template is drawn.

MAPPING

Using the hierarchy of elements and a printout of the package template, the design is mapped. Each element

figure |4-9|

A hierarchy is established from the package elements.

figure |4-10|

Thumbnail sketches help to develop the design.

figure |4-11|

The elements are "mapped" to the various panels, following the hierarchy.

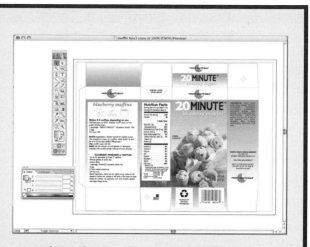

figure |4-12|

The design is transferred to an accurate template on the computer.

figure |4-13|

The printed piece is glued to Bristol board to give the package strength.

is distributed—in word form—across the panels of the package, paying attention to importance, flow, and the logical order of information. This map will serve as a guide in the final design.

Applying the Design to the Template

Following the map, the package panels are designed in proper orientation and scale. At this point, adjustments can be made to be certain the panels work in harmony and that the actual elements will fit well in their assigned space.

Producing the Mock-up

Once the design is fully applied to the template, it's time to make a mock-up to see and feel how well the package performs. Up to this point, most of the work has been on paper or on screen, but a mock-up will allow the package to be held in the hand, viewed from different angles and distances, and placed alongside competing packaging.

A good-quality print is made of the flat package. It's best to print on a surface that will closely approximate the final production of the product; if the actual piece will be made from coated (shiny) paperboard, be sure to print the mock-up on glossy paper.

The print is glued to a sheet of Bristol board. This will give the mock-up the rigidity of the real package. Rubber cement or spray mount is used.

(continued)

Case Study (continued)

figure |4-14|

All fold lines are scored.

figure |4-15|

The package is cut, folded, and assembled.

With a Scoring Tool firmly score along all fold lines. A light table makes it possible to score the paper along the back of the fold (as described in Chapter 2).

Turning the mounted print faceup, the pattern is cut with a sharp X-Acto knife all the way around its perimeter. Care is taken to accurately follow the pattern indications so that tuck flaps fit as designed and corners meet cleanly.

The package is then folded along the score lines and formed into its three-dimensional shape. Paper glue or double-sided tape is applied where indicated—in this case, only three surfaces require adhesive. Again, it is important to follow the plan that the final piece will take in production, both for authenticity and as a trial run to double-check the structural integrity of the design.

figure |4-16|

The finished prototype. (© Chuck Groth)

PROFILE

Morana Rodanovic

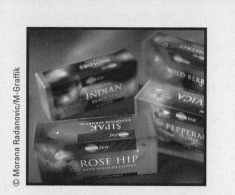

© Morana Radanovic/M-Graffik

In the heart of southeastern Europe, not far from the Adriatic Sea, designer Morana Radanovic produces packaging for an assortment of clients almost as diverse as the markets for which she creates. Morana's design work for m-graffik is distributed throughout Europe and, recently, imported into the United States, . This poses challenges, not only in trying to identifying a target audience, but in such basic elements as language and alphabet. "Croatia was part of Yugoslavia—a market of 24 million inhabitants," she explains. "Since 1991, we spent several years in a war for independence. We became independent, but Croatia has only 4.5 million inhabitants. Therefore, the other former Yugoslav countries are important for market expansion. Now, we have to deal with four similar but different languages (plus, sometimes English), two different alphabets [Cyrillic for Serbia and Montenegro and Macedonia, Latin for Bosnia, Croatia, and the rest of Europe]. We have to struggle with different food laws, endless lines of declarations and usage instructions—while still trying not to jeopardize the packaging's main message."

About her start in package design, Radanovic says, "In the late 1980s, I started work in a design studio in Samobor, near Zagreb. My first real assignment was Christmas packaging for pralines. It was the middle of summer, and I had just come from vacation. The rest of the world was still sunny and warm while I was surrounded by sparkling snowflakes, reindeer and jingle-bells. Living in parallel worlds is probably the reason why, after all this years, I still love designing.

"The first step in any packaging assignment is to get to know my target group. Knowing, understanding, and loving its habits, values, motives, and taste is helpful as I try to create their world around me."

While Radanovic and m-graffik works extensively with large, international clients, the size of the studio has never held them back—in fact, m-graffik is familiar with professional acclaim. "It is a small agency," Radanovic explains, "12 employees, five of them designers. Our core business is, of course, packaging, but also other parts of marketing.

"For Coca-Cola Beverages, we created the two-tenth liter glass bottles for Cappy juices (the European version of Minute Maid) as well as full packaging redesign of eleven tetrabricks for the same product. The two-tenth liter glass bottle created in 2000 won the National and World Packaging Award.

"For Unilever, we created Rama margarine with yogurt packaging, and for Croatian producers we've designed packaging for fruit yogurt, teas, instant drinks, cereals, chocolates, pralines, biscuits, and frozen pastry packaging."

m-graffik is located in Zagreb, Croatia. You can visit them on the Web at www.mgraffik.com. ■

THE UBIQUITOUS LITTLE BOX

figure | 4-17 |

Nutrition facts information can be found in all food and beverage products sold in the U.S.

Sometimes, when studying geological history, scientists come across evidence of environment-altering events, such as those that ushered in the extinction of the dinosaurs.

Interestingly, those looking back through the strata that form the history of package design can point to several comparable events that changed the world of packaging: the discovery of food preservation and canning, the invention of the cardboard box, advancements in printing technologies—each had significant impacts on the field. But one of the most impressive changes took place between 1991 and 1994—a short, three-year period in which virtually every food and beverage package sold in the United States was redesigned.

What brought about this large-scale shake-up? For many years, manufacturers were not held accountable to claims made on packaging for a product's effectiveness or ingredients. Eventually, the United States Food and Drug Administration (FDA) began to enact measures to protect consumers, including displaying accurate net weights of products and prohibiting packages from making untrue health claims. In 1990, the FDA and the U.S. Department of Agriculture passed the *Nutrition Labeling and Education Act,* which required, by 1994, all foods and beverages to list complete and accurate nutritional information in a standardized chart under the heading "Nutrition Facts." This small, ubiquitous graphic, rarely measuring over 2" by 4", altered the face of package design nationwide. This simple addition required modifying all the other elements—graphics, typography, and their scale and arrangements—to accommodate its placement on the food package.

SUMMING IT UP

The mock-up and production flats play important roles in package design. Lending a tangible element to the design process, each serves as a hands-on model for the finished work.

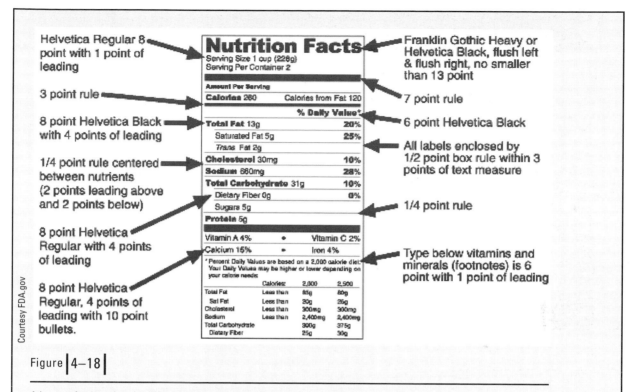

Helvetica Regular 8 point with 1 point of leading

3 point rule

8 point Helvetica Black with 4 points of leading

1/4 point rule centered between nutrients (2 points leading above and 2 points below)

8 point Helvetica Regular with 4 points of leading

8 point Helvetica Regular, 4 points of leading with 10 point bullets.

Franklin Gothic Heavy or Helvetica Black, flush left & flush right, no smaller than 13 point

7 point rule

6 point Helvetica Black

All labels enclosed by 1/2 point box rule within 3 points of text measure

1/4 point rule

Type below vitamins and minerals (footnotes) is 6 point with 1 point of leading

Courtesy FDA.gov

Figure |4–18|

A how-to for creating the "Nutrition Facts" graphic required for all foods and beverages sold in the U.S.
Source: The Food and Drug Administration (www.fda.gov)

Some manufacturers merely scaled down the rest of the labeling. But for many, the new requirement provided the opportunity to readdress some of the visual entrenchments and conventions that manufacturers, designers, marketers, and consumers had been clinging to.

The Facts

The FDA has very specific guidelines for producing the Nutrition Facts box, from type point sizes, to typefaces allowed, to line weights required between listings. In addition to the client's information the designer should be aware of some of the basic traits of the box so he or she can produce it, with the given data, from scratch.

The mock-up is essential for testing structure, flow of information, and the feel of the piece. Use them as design tools, and work will be more rich and communicative. A well-produced flat will serve as an instruction manual when it comes time to print and assemble the actual packaging, and may help to avoid some headaches later on.

CREATING A VIRTUAL MOCK-UP

Designer: Monghan William Wu / Slide photographer: Michael Bodycomb

figure |4-19|

A mock-up does not have to be simple or low-tech; this designer built a custom wooden box as his prototype.

Courtesy PVServices.com

figure |4-20|

An interactive digital "mock-up."

A 3-D modeling mock-up for presentation and design exploration

There are times when it's not cost-effective or even preferable to create a physical mock-up for presentation to a client. Clients may have several offices in different cities—or continents—that need to see the presentation at the same time. Or perhaps creating a form as a design exploration will be too costly or time-consuming. For the package designer, 3-D modeling software can help develop the perfect presentation or determine how a particular design will work on a package without actually constructing it.

If familiar with 3-D modeling software, the designer can create these types of presentations at his or her workstation. If not, there are companies that can produce these virtual mock-ups quickly and affordably. One such company, Product Visualization Services (www. pvservices.com) works from flat package designs to create 3-D digital renderings. They serve as excellent exploration tools for experimenting with form and design, and can be shared with clients and focus groups anywhere in the world. These models can also be rendered as still images for print presentations or portfolios.

How a Virtual Mock-up Works

Virtual mock-ups are 3-D representations of the package design. With these computer presentations, the viewer can click to change views, angles, and zoom in or out on a three-dimensional rendering of a package. The advantages: These models can be viewed by any number of people at the same time, making it easy to share ideas and input; clients and designers can interact with these virtual mock-ups, viewing them from any side or angle, and changes or alterations to the design can be represented quickly.

Courtesy PVServices.com

figure |4-21|

Here, I worked with Product Visualization Services (www.pvservices.com) to create virtual mock-ups of two of the Case Study projects in this book—the 20-MINUTE Muffin Mix box and the RETROGLYPHS wall art package.

in review

1. What purposes does the 3-D mock-up serve in package design?

2. What are the two kinds of 3-D mock-ups? What distinguishes each?

3. Why is a production flat included when files are sent to print?

exercises

1. In pencil, design a package for a series of five identically sized and shaped objects, such as five dice or five golf balls. Make up your own logo, product name, and package text.

2. Using Bristol board, construct a Sketch Model from your design concept in Exercise 1. Draw on the sides to see how the various elements interact across the panels.

3. Transfer your design ideas to your computer. Develop a template for your package structure and print and construct a 3-D Prototype.

4. Assemble a focus group of friends, colleagues, or family. Without directing the group with statements of your own, present the prototype and record the group's reactions and comments. Are they what you expected?

5. Make a production flat for the package. Go through the checklist of elements to determine how thorough and informational the flat is.

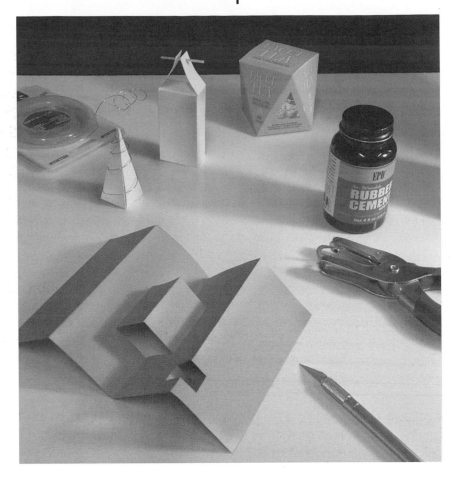

CHAPTER

"When we approach a new package project, the first question we ask ourselves is, 'How can we do this differently?' We're not looking for the obvious solution. We're looking for the creative one."

Sol Lang, Creative Director Crayon Design Group

Chapter Objectives

Introduce several common processes used in the enhancement of packaging

Become familiar with in-studio techniques for reproducing the production processes of:

- **Die cutting**
- **Embossing**
- **Perforations**
- **Pop-ups**
- **Special closures**

Introduction

There are an array of effects and processes available to the designer for enhancing the form, structure, and surface of a package. In professional production, these processes are achieved with special dies, inks, or folds, using dedicated machinery, but many of the effects can be inexpensively duplicated or mimicked in the studio for realistic mock-ups. Learning and using these techniques carries the mock-up to a higher level of professional presentation, allowing designer and client to see a more faithful model

© CHRW Advertising, LLC

figure │5-1│

A simple die cut edge adds movement and life to this niche-market soap package.

of the finished piece. And in mass-production, employing these processes can help a product stand out from its competition—the ultimate goal of packaging—and add to the expressive capabilities of the design.

Studio Techniques

Duplicating various production techniques in the studio permits the designer to not only present the client with a more finished mock-up, but allows for greater exploration and more creative treatment of structure and surface. The following processes are common in the package design field, and should be in the repertoire of anyone desiring to create convincing and innovative designs and 3-D mock-ups.

© Mark Weisz Design

figure |5-2|

These packages use die cuts to engage the viewer, reinforce design, and allow the contents inside the package to play a role in communication.

Die cutting is an integral part of packaging. In fact, almost every paperboard package not formed from a rectangular piece of board uses some sort of die cutting, since the outline of the package template is usually stamped out as a die cut before assembly.

Die Cuts

Essentially, a die cut is like a cookie cutter for paperboard or cardboard. A metal die is formed and usually set into a wooden base. These dies can be fashioned to cut almost any shape, and the process continues to improve with the implementation of computer-aided die systems and laser cutter technology.

After printing, the board is passed through the die press and the shapes are cut. More complex die cuts may require several passes through various dies before the piece is finished.

The die cut window in a package serves several functions: it adds a compelling visual element, bringing negative space into the design; it draws the audience into the package by

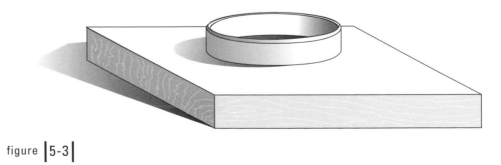

figure |5-3|

The typical cutting die is composed of a formed blade set into a wooden base.

introducing a component of layering and depth; and it allows textures, surfaces, and information normally hidden by the packaging to come through into view. A thoughtful die cut will take all of its potential strengths into consideration. The designer should ask, "Is this die cut necessary? Is it creating a strong element within the overall design? Does it engage the viewer in a way not possible without the cut? Does the cut reveal relevant and interesting information inside the package?"

To produce a die cut in the studio, the only tools required are a sharp X-Acto knife and a cutting mat. When applying the design to the package template, indicate the die cut shape and where it will be placed (this is also important when producing the production flat). Print the package and affix it to Bristol or other substrate for strength and rigidity. With a very sharp blade, cut the shape from the package. If the cuts are to be straight, no other guide than a metal ruler is necessary. If the die cut is to be curved, it's a good idea to practice cutting curves on a piece of scrap material. Work until curves can be cut cleanly and smoothly. I warm up by cutting various diameter circles and "S" curves.

One thing to note when employing die cuts: Be sure the cut does not compromise the strength of the package. Overcutting can weaken the panels and cause them to be flimsy—sometimes to the point of sagging.

© Graphical House

figure |5-4|

Graphical House (London) used die cuts to add depth, texture, and information to this package for Lemon Zester Soap. In this case, the die cut serves both as a strong design element and as a device to draw the audience to the soap within the box.

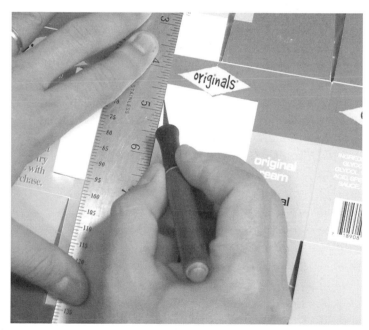

figure |5-5|

A sharp knife and a cutting mat are the only tools needed to add a die cut to an in-studio mock-up.

PROFILE

Steve Smith

© Tazo

Steve Smith decided to start a specialty tea company in the United States—a country not particularly known for tea drinking—at a time when the coffee craze was just beginning to move like a wave across the nation. "Why would I start a tea company," Smith asked himself, "when there were already a lot of teas out there occupying shelf space and the category was pretty mature? I felt that there was a customer waiting out there for a more interesting tea experience, and that not only meant taste, but how we could get one to connect with tea in a way that they've never done before."

Smith understood that succeeding in a crowded field meant presenting the product in a package that would speak to his market. "You can create pretty packaging and get somebody to buy a product the first time," he says, "but have them turn away from your product for a repeat purchase because it doesn't deliver on the promise. Packaging has been so critical to this brand because it communicates premium in a way that no other tea package has been able to do. It 'pops' due to its restraint. This packaging has done a lot of heavy lifting for us—last year was the first year that we've done any consumer advertising, and that's almost ten years into this project.

"Let me tell you how the idea of Tazo came about. Initially, when I was with Stash Tea, I had wanted to develop a retail tea concept. I worked with a designer, and she and I had conceptualized an environment

Embossing

Embossing is the process of raising certain portions of a paper or board to achieve a three-dimensional effect. In commercial production, embossing is done by creating a set of two opposing dies—a male die and a female die—between which the substrate is pressed under pressure. The result is a raised image. When the raised image is combined with ink, it is called a stamped emboss; if the image is not inked and is defined solely by the different levels of the paper, it is known as a blind emboss. Either way, the effect can be subtle, sophisticated, and eye-catching.

© Tazo

that we described as "a little bit Merlin, a little bit Marco Polo and a little bit 'Raiders of the Lost Ark'—this mélange of cultures. We took that template that we did in 91–92 and I carted it over to [designer Steve] Sandstrom. You know, it's about the architecture of the packaging, what it looks like, but it's really the voice of the packaging and the voice of the brand—when we applied the voice to the packaging, it all started to come together. Co-founder Steve Sandos described it best when he said, "It [the packaging] shouldn't feel like it's from 'here and now,' but like it's from 'there and then.'

"Working with Steve Sandstrom has been a great education for me. Now I see when a designer crowds a package or the type spacing is all screwy or they're trying to do too much. There's a hierarchy with packaging, and we try to manage that.

"I briefed them on my thinking—a starting point—and it was really the Three Steves [Steve Smith, copywriter and co-founder Steve Sandos, and package designer Steve Sandstrom] sitting around and talking about what tea could be, how we could change the perception of tea as a beverage and revitalize the category. As we talked about these things, Steve Sandstrom started sketching, as he always does, and he felt at the time that maybe the logo TAZO should be not just letters, but symbols. So he found a type font, broke it up a bit, and after putting the font together into the logo, we looked at it and said, 'that's it.'

Smith has worked to be certain the product measures up to the promise of the packaging. "Our brand is appealing to a lot of people—it's very egalitarian—it doesn't leave people out," he explains. "It's smart without looking down on people. The success of what we've done has got everything to do with the packaging and the 'voice' for trial, and the quality of the product is what's kept people coming back."

Steve Smith if the founder of TAZO Tea in Portland, Oregon, on the Web at www.tazo.com. ■

There are several ways to duplicate the embossing process in the design studio without expensive die-making machinery or heavy paper presses.

One method is to devise a handmade embossing plate. Work begins by designing the image to be embossed. The paper to be embossed is aligned on a board or plate with registration marks to provide for exact placement. The embossing die is made fairly easily by cutting the image or design from a material of thickness equal to the desired height of the emboss.

| TIPS |

When embossing by hand, it's best not to attempt to raise the image too high in relation to the rest of the paper; the embossed effect is achieved by actually stretching the paper fibers, and trying to overdo it may tear or distort the work.

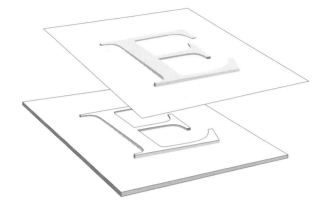

figure |5-6|

Create an embossing plate by raising desired elements above the plate surface. Then, either carefully burnish the paper over the plate by hand or run the paper and plate through a wheel press.

The embossing die is placed in position on the plate and the printed work is laid over the board and held in position. At this point, the work may be run through a wheel press, if one is available, or the designer may use a stylus to rub around the embossing template to stretch the paper around it. A smooth, rounded stylus is best to reduce the likelihood of tearing. It may take several attempts before an adequate emboss is achieved, but the process is quick enough to allow for experimentation.

| SURVEY |

What tools do you use most frequently?

Computer keyboard and mouse	**48%**
Pen or pencil and paper	**43%**
Brush and paper or canvas	**12%**

Totals shown may be more or less than 100% due to rounding.

SOURCE: The International Council of Graphic Design Associations

Another technique for embossing involves thermographic ink. Thermographic ink is ink that reacts to heat by melting and expanding. Supplies required for this procedure include clear embossing ink, embossing powder (available in many colors), a small watercolor brush, an erasable ballpoint pen, and an embossing heat gun—all of which are readily available at most stationery and hobby shops. In this method, the printed design is placed flat on a clean work surface. Clear embossing ink is applied to the area to be raised with a brush or a rubber stamp and embossing powder is sprinkled over the area while the ink is still wet. After a moment, the excess powder is poured off. With an embossing heat gun, the applied powder is heated until it melts and expands.

Perforations

The typical box is opened in one of three ways: it is ripped open along a glued set of panels; it is opened at an unsealed junction; or, it is torn open along a perforated edge. A perforated opening is made up of two elements. One is a solid, closed container, joined by glue or other means; the other is a delineated line set apart by a successive series of cuts, holes, or other weakened areas of the substrate that allow it to be easily torn. Everyone is familiar with packages that direct us to "Tear Along Dotted Line" or "Push Tab and Pull Back to Open." These perforated openings allow the consumer to quickly and easily open packaging without damaging the rest of the container unnecessarily. Perforations are accomplished in production by the use of a special die that cuts the slices or dots into the substrate. Much like a scoring or cutting die, the steel perforation die is set up as part of the production process. This effect can be re-created in the studio with simple tools and a little perseverance and planning. You'll need a ruler, a thick sewing needle, and an X-Acto knife.

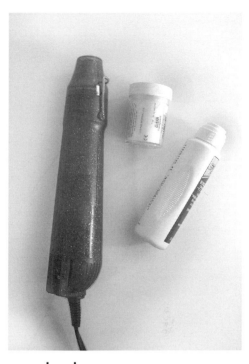

figure | 5-7 |

Embossing can be mimicked with thermographic inks, powders, and a heat gun.

Once the type of perforation is determined, the box is designed in the normal fashion, but the area to be perforated is established on the flat print. Push-and-tear perforations may be reproduced by running the print through a standard sewing machine with an unthreaded needle. The needle will make a series of uniform, evenly spaced holes in the package, which will serve to indicate a perforated opening. With no access to a sewing machine, the holes can be duplicated—albeit painstakingly—with a thick needle and a line guide and poking each hole, one at a time, through the board. Care should be taken in this method that the holes are uniformly spaced and sized.

Another type of perforated opening employs the "Lift-and-Pull" zipper. In this case, instead of a line of holes, the perforation is produced by cutting a successive series of slits along the line to be opened. These slits are often paired in parallel lines so the perforation may be torn as a

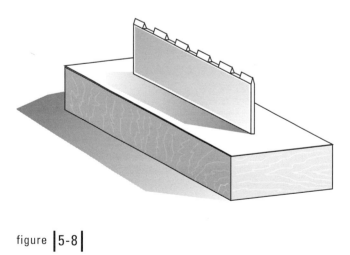

figure | 5-8 |

A commercial perfing die makes a uniform series of cuts in the paper or board.

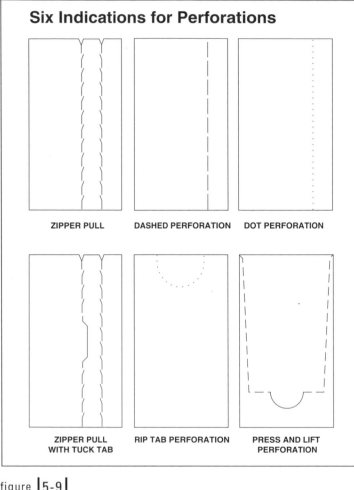

Six Indications for Perforations

ZIPPER PULL   DASHED PERFORATION   DOT PERFORATION

ZIPPER PULL WITH TUCK TAB   RIP TAB PERFORATION   PRESS AND LIFT PERFORATION

figure |5-9|

Six different perforation styles for paperboard packaging.

strip in "zipper" fashion along the opening. In this case, a series of X-Acto knife cuts defines the perforation. A slender line of glue outside the edge of the perforation seals the panels.

Pop-ups

Another interesting variation sometimes found in the package structure is the use of pop-ups and other movable sections. Pop-ups add a sense of surprise to a design, are often playful and fun, and can help a piece become more interactive. Types of pop-ups or movable elements include simple, expanding folds, and more complex pop-ups with multiple pieces and informational wheels that can be turned to reveal different bits of information through a fixed window. Each of these adds a component of motion and works to engage the viewer, but at a fairly high expense; all pop-ups must be hand-assembled, making them labor intensive and costly. They should be reserved for special circumstances when the pop-up is really appropriate and when their 3-D aspect can communicate information better than a flat or static image.

In production, pop-ups are another application of the die-cutting process. And just like other die cuts, pop-ups can be produced in the studio with simple equipment such as an X-Acto knife, paper glue, and grommets and grommet-setting tools. Each pop-up—basic or complex—requires a good deal of planning, experimentation, and trial-and-error investigation. So much so, in fact, that the popular name for professional pop-up design is "paper engineering." The best way to learn the craft is to gather an assortment of pop-up examples, from greeting cards to books, and do a little "reverse engineering" by disassembling them and discovering their principles. The following figures, however, illustrate three basic techniques.

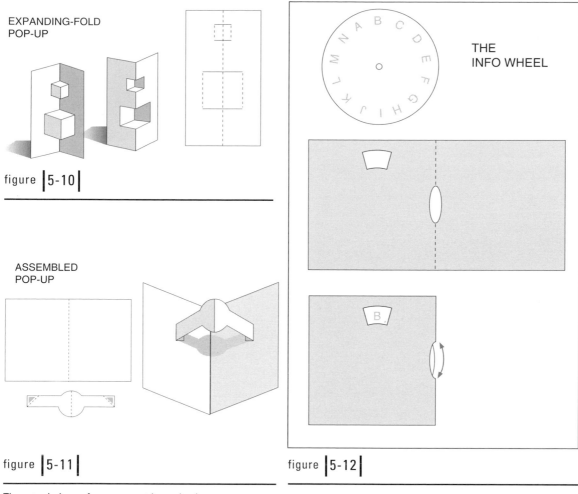

EXPANDING-FOLD
POP-UP

figure | 5-10 |

ASSEMBLED
POP-UP

figure | 5-11 |

THE
INFO WHEEL

figure | 5-12 |

Three techniques for pop-up art in packaging:
- The Expanding Fold
- The Info Wheel
- The Assembled Pop-up

Special Closures

Most packages are closed and sealed by gluing overlapping panels, interlocking tuck flaps, or nesting a lid over a base. But there are other methods for sealing that can add to the visual and tactile experience of a package design.

Although the variations are infinite, here are a few examples to explore the possibilities. Each of these can be duplicated easily in a handmade mock-up with readily obtainable supplies.

figure | 5-13 |

Devising special closures can add unique, eye-catching elements to otherwise simple packaging.

Case Study

Using Special Processes in a Mock-up for Presentation: Die Cut and Expanding Fold Pop-up

The Problem

To design a package for a cosmetic cream and a "free gift" sample fragrance bottle. The cream is an established brand, but the fragrance is new. The package should attract regular and new customers and draw attention to the new product.

Hierarchy

All the elements that must appear on the package are listed and ranked in order of their importance and function. Once the hierarchy is established, the design begins.

Initial Design

The designer creates some early thumbnail designs. Initially, the sample was going to be inside the cream packaging, but later ideas found that it would be more effective to bring it outside the box, to highlight it and demand more attention.

Ideas are developed and a plan is made to employ a die cut window to reveal the cream inside the box, and a pop-up fold holder to display the fragrance outside the box.

Designing a New Template

Since the concept of this design is different from the rest of the product line, a new design template must be created. Pencil sketches help to determine placement of the die cut and pop-up, and an accurate template is developed on the computer.

figure |5-14|

Hand cream and fragrance sample need new packaging.

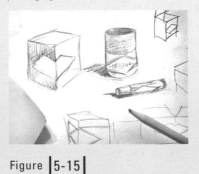

Figure |5-15|

Thumbnails develop the concept of using special processes in the package structure.

figure |5-16|

Pencil sketches aid in envisioning the flat pattern of the package.

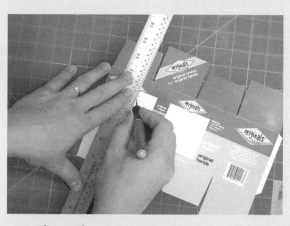

figure | 5-17 |

Die cut and pop-up are cut during the assembly of the mock-up.

figure | 5-18 |

The mock-up is ready for presentation.

Producing the Mock-up with Die Cut and Opposing-Fold Pop-up

The new design is applied to the packaging template. Special attention is given to indicate the die cut and pop-up, since these are unusual elements for this product line and will need to be executed by hand in the mock-up.

A quality print is made and glued to Bristol board to approximate the paperboard weight of the final package. As in other mock-ups, the design is scored at the fold lines and cut at the perimeter.

With a very sharp X-Acto knife, the die cut is cut as cleanly as possible with the X-Acto, following the indicated line. Also with the X-Acto, the pop-up is cut where shown and the proper folds are made to make the pop-up come out and away from the box, leaving a pocket for the fragrance sample.

The box is folded and assembled. The products are placed in the box and pop-up to double-check the accuracy of their positions.

© Paguirigan Branding Design

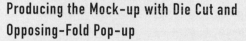

figure | 5-19 |

The die-cut collars for these Ensante Vinaigrette bottles bring a dynamic quality to a familiar shape.

PROFILE

Cherie Fister

Cherie Fister, an Associate Professer of Graphic Design, teaches packaging to about eighty undergrad students at Maryville University in St. Louis. Fister describes the school as one "dedicated to the liberal arts and selected professional programs." She believes the general education opportunities of a liberal arts college give her students exposures to a world beyond design. "Students of visual communication need to be well educated in their discipline (design, craft, technology, tradition)," she says, "but without a sense of context, of culture, they have less than a full command of the design process. I think they have a stronger chance of becoming insightful, innovative, thoughtful designers when their professional studies are companioned by forays into psychology, language, science, history, and literature.

"I teach an introduction to packaging & presentation course to junior-level students. My job is to develop their awareness of the omnipresence of packaging and other three-dimensional promotional design. What do volume, scale, tactility, economy, shipping concerns, modular design, shelf-space wars and the precious but limited attention span of a customer bring to the design puzzle?"

Fister stresses the importance of expanding the learning milieu beyond the walls of the university. "Each major project, whether it's a package or a venture into point-of-purchase design, begins outside the classroom," she explains. "This may bring the class to food markets, shopping malls, or boutique shops. An assessment of the environment, the competition and the targeted client informs every design decision. I may point out current design trends, but the goal is to teach students to observe, research and then evaluate the ever-changing elements of style." Taking the teaching directly into the marketplace not only reinforces concepts, but involves the student in the process of discovery in their real-world application.

"A dynamically designed, well-crafted container is the primary goal, but the final measure of success—will a native of the chosen county recognize the source of the imagery and smile?"

When Cherie Fister came to Maryville seven years ago, the graphic design program was a fledgling off-shoot of the rest of the art department. Since then, it's grown each year to its present size of eighty students, from both freshman enrollment and growing numbers of transfer students.

"My experience in teaching packaging leads me to conclude that competence in 3 dimensional design can in almost all cases be learned (though for some it is a truly mysterious journey). The natively gifted packaging student, however, usually makes their talent apparent in the first mock-up."

You can email Cherie at cfister@maryville.edu. ∎

Case Study

Designing a Package for an Art Object

The Problem

To design a package for a RETROGLYPHS Distinctive Wall Art Sun Spiral wall hanging. RETROGLYPHS is a company producing wall art in bas-relief, reminiscent of ancient art. The wall art is suitable for indoor or outdoor display. The audience is middle- to upper-income consumers with disposable income for artwork. The target consumer enjoys nature and may enjoy displaying unique objects in the home or garden for everyday viewing and while entertaining. The item is also part of a series, so the packaging style should be adaptable to other pieces. These art pieces are to be sold in specialty shops such as garden nurseries, florists, and elite botanical garden gift shops.

The object itself is somewhat heavy, so packaging must accommodate weight. While not fragile, the artwork is breakable if subjected to excessive stress or shock.

figure |5-20|

The wall hanging to be packaged.

Hierarchy

The designer lists the required elements, as determined by the client. The package should show the art object, the RETROGLYPHS logo, item name, company slogan, description of the object, handmade attributes, series description, photo of other objects in the series, barcode (UPC), recycling symbol, and the company address.

Initial Design

A thorough series of thumbnail sketches are produced, experimenting with form and function of the package.

It's decided that the package should have a natural, "crate-like" appearance, as you might see at an archeological dig to protect specimens. To emphasize this crate idea, the package is structured to open with a lid that will reveal the art object nestled inside.

One design is chosen, and additional, more detailed sketches are produced. A packaging template is created on the computer, using an illustration program.

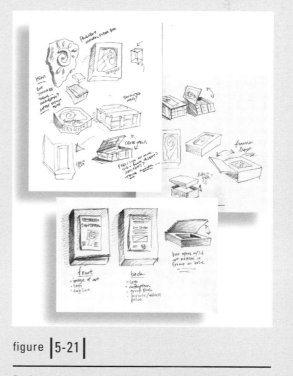

figure |5-21|

Design concepts are explored in pencil sketches.

(continued)

Case Study (continued)

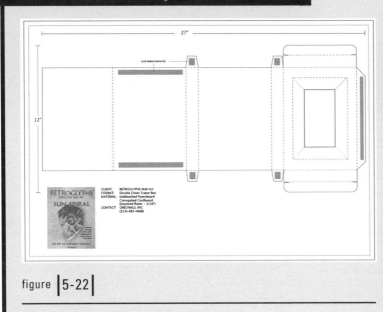

figure |5-22|

The design is applied to the digital template.

figure |5-23|

The completed 3-D prototype mock-up.

Mapping

Using the hierarchy of elements and a printout of the package template, the design is mapped. Working with the client, the designer decides to have the front and back information appear like labels on a crate or other natural box.

Applying Design to the Template

Following the map, the information is distributed between the front and back, and a design is developed. A decision is made to use textured paper to serve as a background, and designed labels are placed in position.

Creating the Mock-up

The package design and template are printed on a good-quality paper and mounted to Bristol board. The package is cut, scored, and assembled. A natural fiber moss is added for packing around the wall art. This serves not only to protect the piece in shipping, but to add another level of authenticity to the archeological theme of the design. The wall art is packed into the mock-up, and it's ready to present to client.

SUMMING IT UP

By introducing extra processes and effects, the package designer carries a piece beyond an ordinary box to a truly expressive and communicative mock-up for the client. Many processes, which

The Production Flat Is Produced

The flat design and template are printed, noting all production information, such as the special "framing" fold of the box interior, all typefaces and photographic images used, paperboard specifications, and designer contact information. This is mounted to a piece of mounting board.

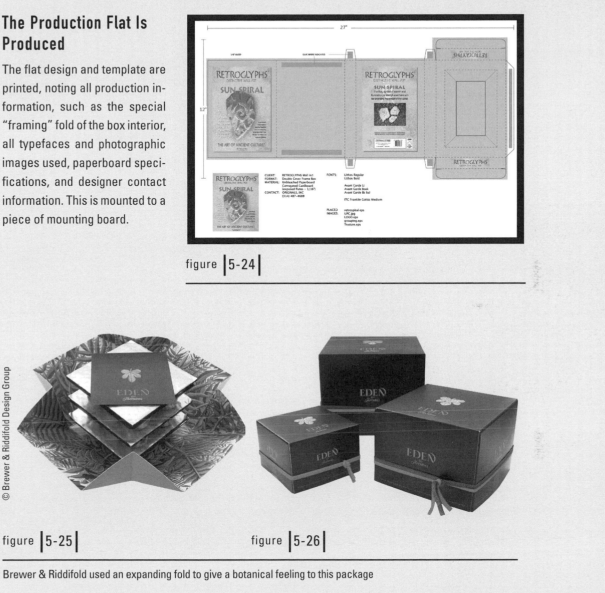

figure | 5-24 |

figure | 5-25 | figure | 5-26 |

Brewer & Riddifold used an expanding fold to give a botanical feeling to this package

are complex and expensive in production, can be replicated in the studio at little cost for these one-offs, and give a more accurate representation of the final vision for the package design. This chapter sought to introduce a small number of these techniques. There are many more to explore, and each will elevate the craft and enhance the studio mock-up.

in review

1. What are some of the production processes that can be replicated in the design studio?

2. When considering a die cut for a package, what are the questions a designer should ask?

3. What are the two types of embossing? What might be the advantages and limitations of each?

4. What similarity does the perforation have with other production processes?

5. When would a pop-up be a good choice for a package? Why is this production process so expensive?

exercises

1. Draw a series of different diameter circles and various trapezoids on paperboard or cardboard. With a sharp X-Acto knife, cut them out as cleanly as you can. Repeat this exercise until you can create accurate die cuts with precision.

2. Make an embossing plate. In this exercise, create a variety of images to be embossed, from very simple to complex. Practice embossing on several different types of paper or board.

3. Find as many packages with perforations as you can. Create a sketch of the different perforation patterns along with a written description of how each functions.

4. Three simple pop-up techniques were described in this chapter. Reproduce each. Find at least one package or promotional piece that uses a form of pop-up.

5. Special closures are most often found on unique, niche-market packages. Why might that be? Examine how the costs of these more involved closures can be justified in package design.

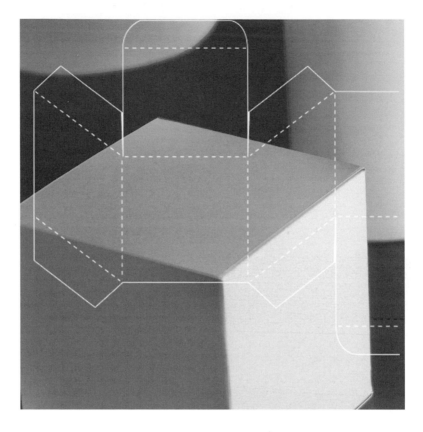

CHAPTER

"Young designers need to spend more time researching, experimenting and executing their projects. They must be serious about what they are doing and focus on the future. I expect new, fresh and creative ideas for packaging design from them. Take a look at creative package design out there and learn how the structure was created."

Tadashi Isozaki

Chapter Objectives

Think 3-D, work 2-D

Choose the appropriate structure for your package

Introduction

The concept of paperboard packaging owes a great deal to the work of Brooklyn bagmaker and printer Robert Gair. His development of the folded cardboard box in the 1870s revolutionized the packaging and package design industries with his idea of using a series of dies to score and cut paper or cardboard in one operation, which produced the world's first ready-to-assemble foldable cartons. Before this, cartons were cut, folded, and glued by hand—a painstaking process—and stored in warehouses awaiting use. This replaced a system marked by slow and expensive production and inefficiency—an empty carton took up as much space as a filled carton, leading to high shipping and storage costs. With the folding cardboard box, packaging could be printed, cut, scored, and shipped flat, then assembled and filled as needed.

Today, cardboard packaging can take almost any form, from simple, one-piece folded boxes to elaborate and intricate origami-inspired works of paper art.

ENVISIONING PATTERNS

The design of any structure, whether it's a home, a warehouse, or a shoebox, begins with understanding what it will be used for, what it will hold, and the aesthetic goals of the project. In the example of a home, the architect must ask, "Will this be a no-frills

figure |6-1|

The folded cardboard box is easy and inexpensive to produce.

residence, or will it include a home office or recreational space? How many people will be living in the space? And what lifestyle will the inhabitants be looking to accommodate?" Not until these questions are answered can the designer determine if the home should be a three-room bungalow, a sprawling ranch, a three-story Tudor, or an efficiency apartment.

figure |6-2|

Sketching on tracing paper is a quick way to explore package shapes.

The same holds true in packaging. Examine the product that will go into the package. Is it fragile? Durable? Oddly shaped? A stackable cube? Is it a solid, liquid, or powder? Each of these factors will determine, to some extent, the form the package will take. Remember: form follows function.

One technique for envisioning the form of a package is to photograph the product and, laying tracing paper over the photo, sketch various package shapes around the product. Will it fit nicely into a cube? Or, is a tall cylinder more appropriate for this product? This method provides for quick, multiple explorations of form.

Once a basic structure is determined for the design, the shape should be sketched in more detail. Pencil, pens, and markers are ideal media at this stage. Working with the dimensional sketch, the artist can roughly visualize each of the panels that will go into the package. Drawing these panels side by side, the sketch is virtually "unwrapped" to see the flat pattern. Careful measurements are made and templates are created.

More Than One Way to Skin a Cat

figure |6-3|

Euclid, born around 325 BC, was the father of modern geometry.

One very important thing to consider when creating package pattern templates is that almost every form can be created in many different ways. Orientation of panels, determination of top and bottom, and where the package will open are all issues to consider. In earlier chapters, several alternatives were discussed for constructing a six-sided cube. Each has specific advantages and attributes that should be taken into account. The same can be said of the other forms. Numerous solutions are possible for most packages; the designer must choose the answer that best suits the need at hand. Each pattern presented in this book is a workable structure to achieve a particular form, but the creative designer will consider them all as starting points, open to reinterpretation and modification.

FORM FOLLOWS FUNCTION

While the following patterns primarily reflect paperboard packaging, it should be restated that package design encompasses containers made from many different materials. Acetate, P.E.T., glass, plastic, foil, tin—the list could go on to name virtually any material that can be used to house a product.

The emphasis has been placed, however, on paperboard for several reasons. First, paperboard or cardboard packaging makes up the vast majority of container work being produced in the field. Its base—wood pulp—is a renewable resource, and recycling extends the reach of that resource more and more each year. Increasingly, designers and manufacturers alike are looking to such reusable materials as cost-effective and environment-friendly choices.

In addition to that, paperboard packaging is the most accessible medium of package design, easily manipulated by hand, in the studio, by a designer or student of package design. Without the ability or equipment to mold glass, metal, or plastic, the studio artist is limited to finding existing packaging and merely relabeling it.

When packaging a product in glass, there are mainly three approaches to applying graphics and information. First, the information may be formed into the glass as either a raised or recessed image. Second, it's possible to print the label information directly onto the glass. Third, and most commonly, a label may be printed separately and glued to the container, as is the case on a wine bottle.

Dealing with metal containers, the same concerns and solutions of glass apply. The metal can be printed, molded, or labeled to suit needs.

P.E.T. or plastic can also be molded to almost any shape, and the possibilities are continually expanding and being refined. The growing trend toward orbital extrusion has allowed for more intricate surface detail on plastic packaging than ever before—in some cases, eliminating the need for additional labeling or printing.

But for the beginning package designer looking to exercise his or her creativity three-dimensionally beyond producing flat labeling for existing containers, paperboard yields endless opportunities and potentials. More than that, most of the concerns addressed in this book have as much relevancy to the other materials as to paperboard.

Economy and Ecology

Attention must be paid to the economical and efficient use of material. Just about every package will require some amount of wasted material, but needlessly using excess packaging is not only costly in production but results in a squandering of resources. More and more designers—and clients—are seeing the benefits of an ecological consideration to package design, not only in terms of lower costs from using less material, but also in public perceptions and acceptance.

Figure | 6-4 |

Common packaging forms.

| SURVEY |

Theoretical research is obviously important in the academic world of design, but is it relevant for practitioners?

Designers with theoretical research skills are better practitioners.

I strongly agree.	**61%**
I agree.	**31%**
I disagree.	**11%**

Totals shown may be more or less than 100% due to rounding.

SOURCE: The International Council of Graphic Design Associations

THE TEMPLATES

Following, you will find four sections of templates for familiar—and not so familiar—packages: square and rectangular boxes, pyramids, cones and cylinders, and unusual shapes.

By far the most commonly used packing form is the cube, or variations thereof. It is versatile, uncomplicated to make, convenient to pack and ship, and easy to display.

Pyramids are considerably less common. It should be noted, however, that because they are less frequently used, they are probably more distinctive and attention getting. There are many ways to construct a pyramid, depending upon the number of sides desired, the size of the base to the height of the sides, and how the designer would like the box to open.

Cylinders, though a familiar form in packaging (think of the canned-goods aisle at your local market), are pretty straightforward to construct. You will find several options here.

Cones are probably among the least frequently used forms. Consisting of a funnel and a base, there is not a lot of variation in their pattern layout, except for the height and base measurements, which determines the angle of the side.

The section of unusual forms is interesting in that it displays some approaches to package construction that vary from the norm. These patterns will show how to lay out and create packages from the slightly off-beat to the intricate and whimsical.

The examples given here are in no way exhaustive representations of what is possible in packaging structure. But an understanding of these will yield more ideas and reinforce the concepts of package templates and 3-D constructions.

BOXES AND CUBES

The six-sided box is by far the most prevalent form in retail and commercial packaging. The sides are usually, but not always, parallelograms, and can be configured in many different ways. In most cases, they consist of two pairs of like-size panels with a top and bottom, which are either glued or tuck-locked.

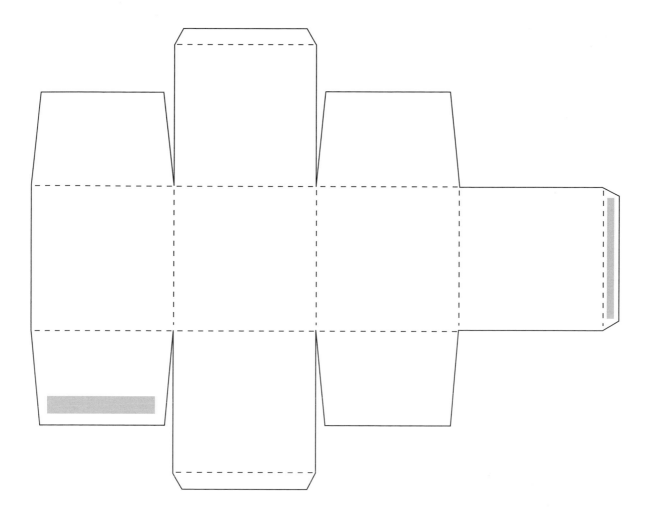

TUCK-FLAP TOP BOX

A common box with tuck-flap top and glued bottom. Dimensions of sides may be easily adjusted.

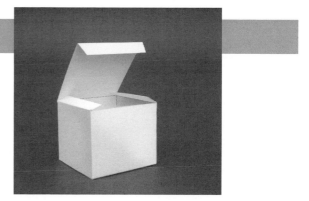

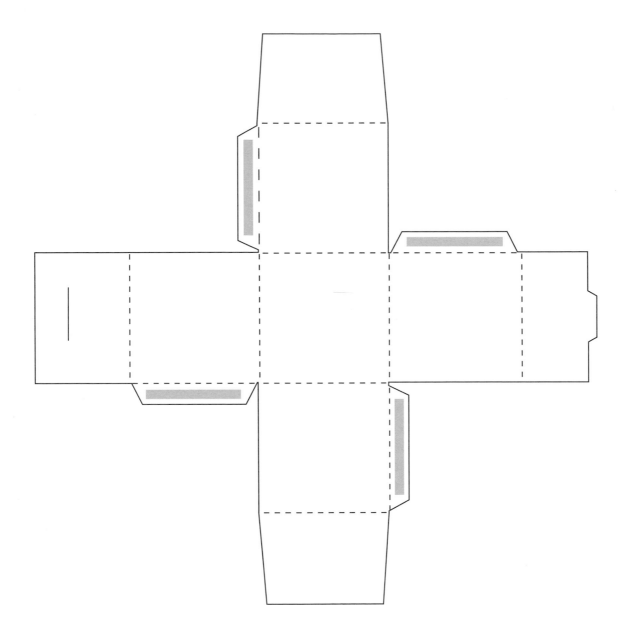

RESEALABLE CUBE

**A basic cube with a
tuck-lock closure top.**

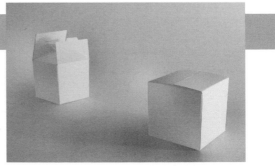

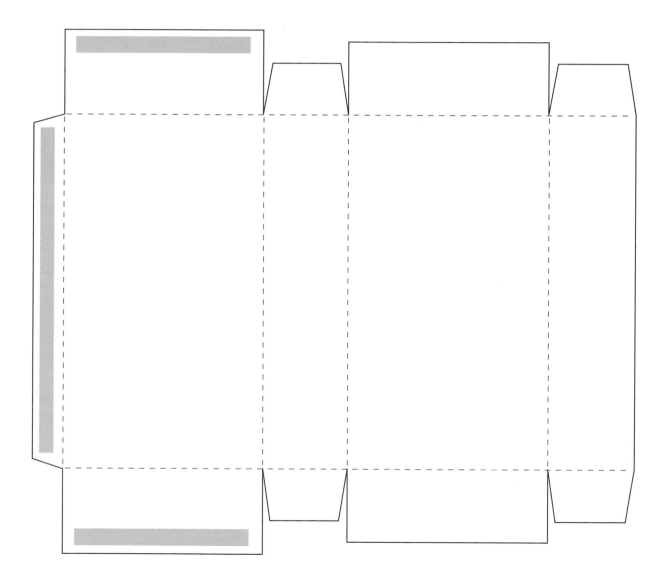

GLUED TOP and BOTTOM BOX

A very basic, glued-end box.
May be combined with
perforations for opening.

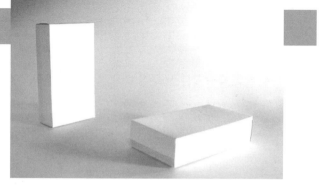

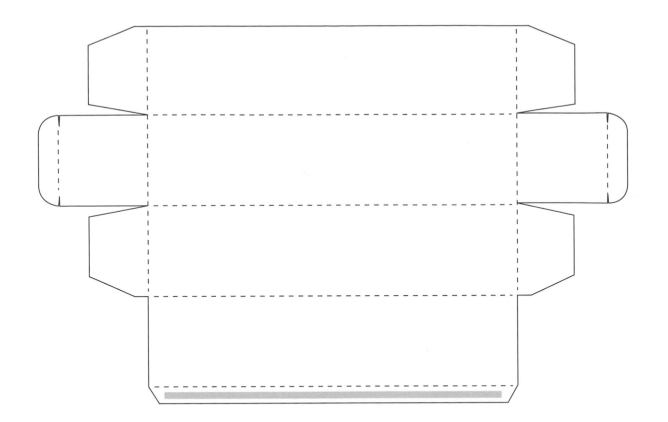

TALL TUCK-FLAP BOX

A simple six-panel box with tuck-flap ends that can be designed with a horizontal or vertical orientation.

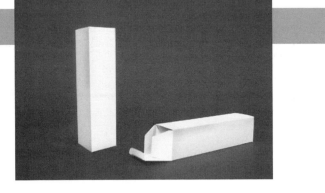

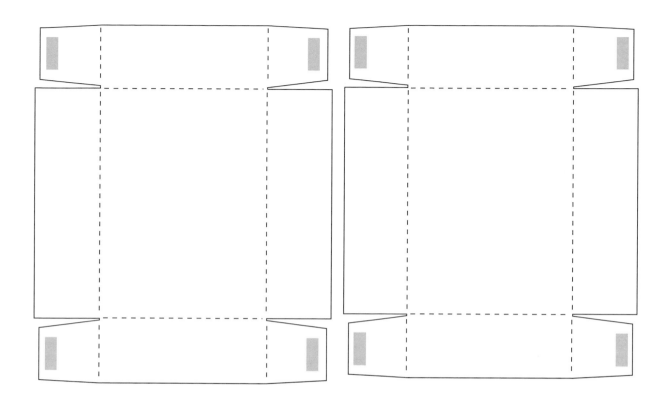

TWO-PIECE GIFT BOX

A basic box consisting of two separate trays—one slightly larger than the other—to make base and lid.

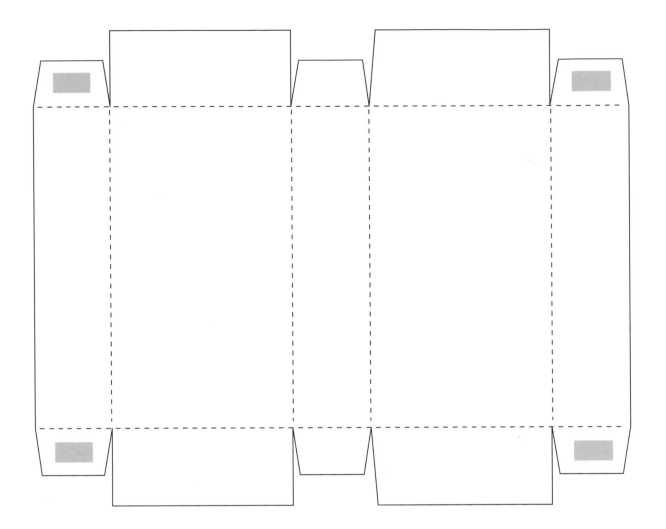

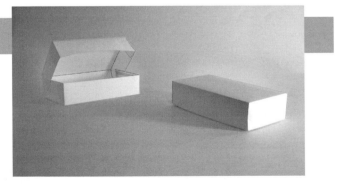

ONE-PIECE FLAT BOX

The attached lid of this box makes it
easy to open with one hand.
The lid slightly overlaps the base.

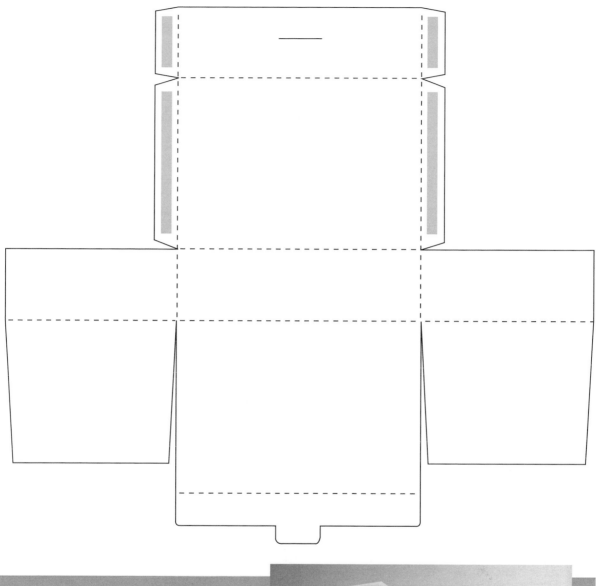

FLAT BOX with TUCK CLOSURE

This one-piece flat box has large top flaps and an attached lid that secures with a tuck closure.

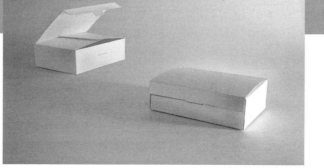

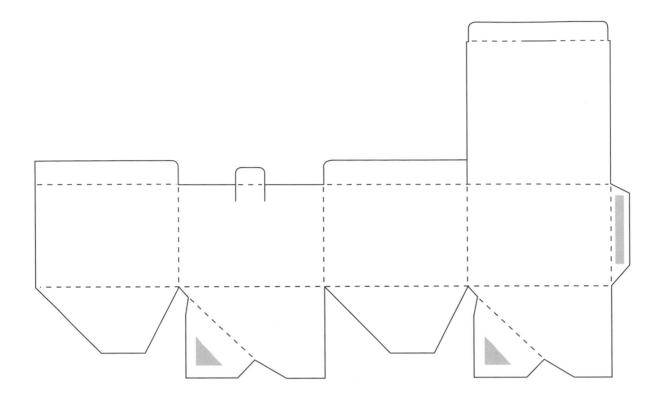

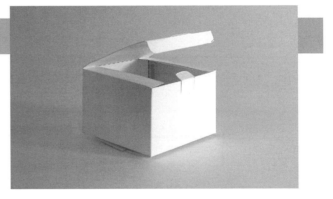

LIDDED CUBE with TUCK-LOCK

The angled tuck-lock adds extra security to this box closure and interlocking flaps strengthen the box base.

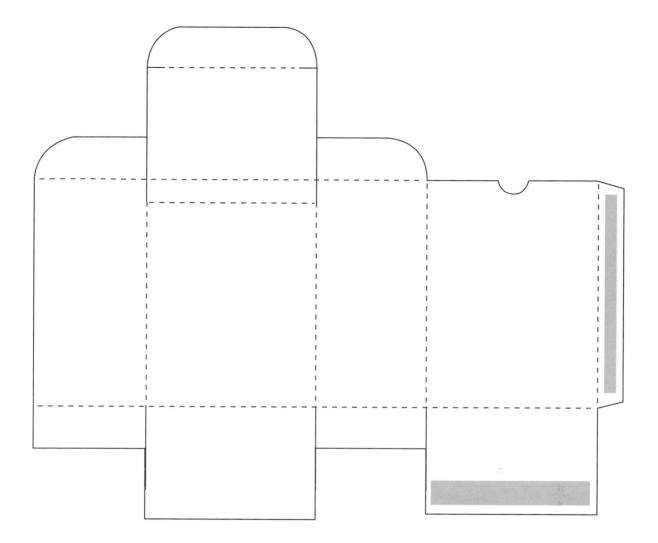

DEEP TUCK BOX

A simple tuck-lid box with a glued bottom for strength. Features a lowered fold back for the lid, allowing the box to have a wider top opening.

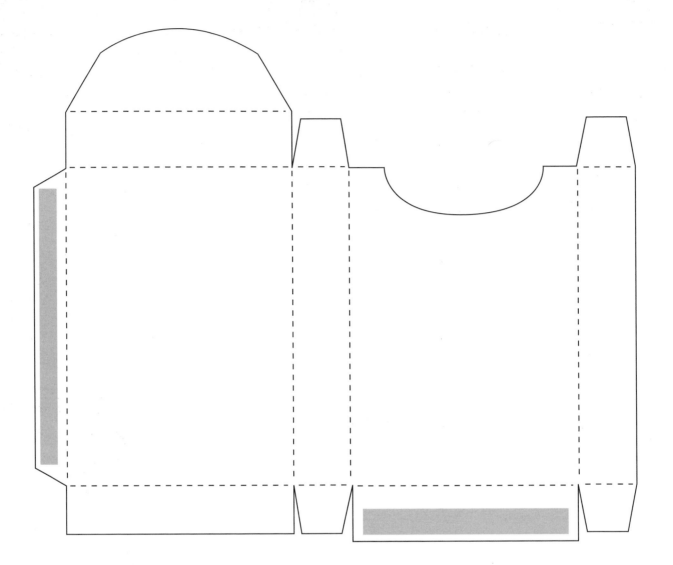

BASIC TUCK BOX

Simple box with a tuck-flap lid. This style of package is typical for containing playing cards, crayons, etc.

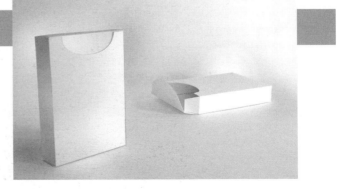

figure |3|

© Graphical House (Glasgow)

figure |4|

Design by Matt Bender

figure 6

figure |7|

© Hornall Anderson Design Works

figure |8|

Package design by Randy Mosher Design
(randymosherdesign.com)

figure |9|

Design by Daniel Shinn

figure |10|

© Boots, Design by AM Associates (London)

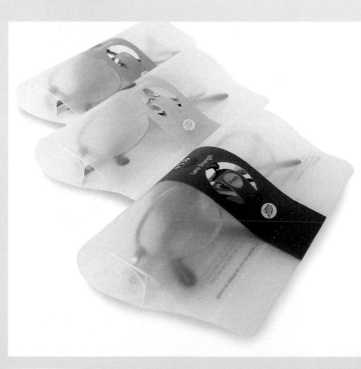

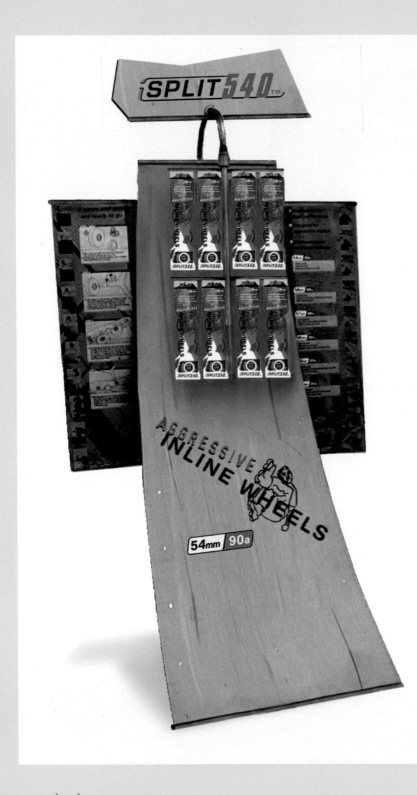

figure |11|

Design by Matt Bender

figure |15|

Package design by Randy Mosher Design (www.randymosherdesign.com)

figure |16|

Design by Pomegranate Design (Photograph by Rob Mandolene)

figure |17|

© Burt's Bees

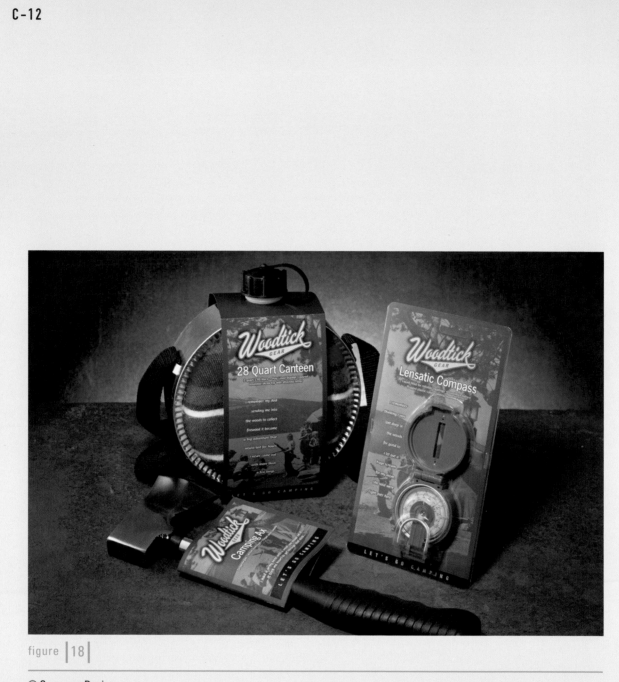

figure |18|

figure |19|

© LPG Design

figure |20|

Design by Jessica McEntire
(Photgraph by Tadashi Isozaki)

The main ingredient in the "mind" tea is Ginko IQ. Ginko IQ specifically prepared to enhance mental performance. Ginko helps stimulate cerebral circulation by refreshing brain cells with an abundance of blood and oxygen. Ginko will leave also help to improve focal and concentration skills.

mind

The main ingredient in the "body" tea is ginseng which helps boost mental and physical energy. It improves blood circulation to the heart, increases reaction time, balances cholesterol and blood sugar, overall leaving you more energized by stimulating central nervous system.

body

figure │21│

Design by Jessica McEntire (Photgraph by Tadashi Isozaki)

figure │22│

Design by Dmitry Paperny

figure |23|

Design by Bradford Klemmer (Photo by Tadashi Isozaki)

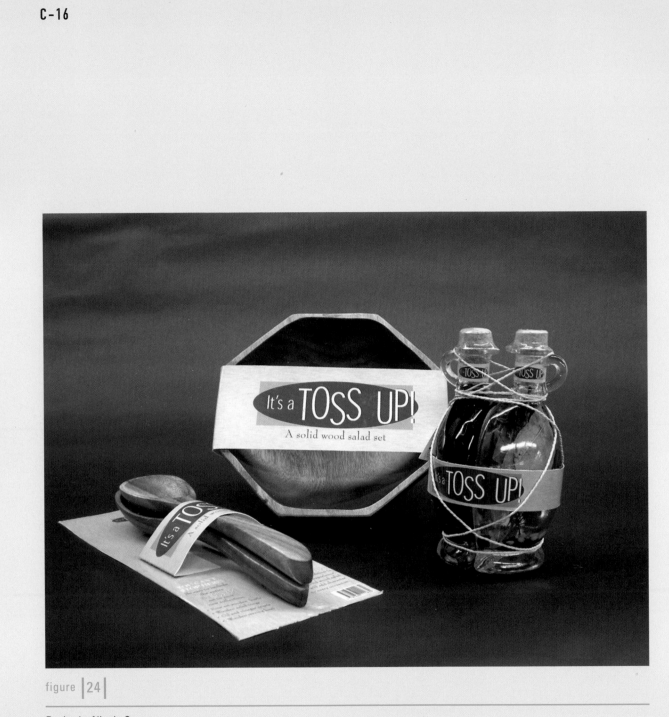

figure |24|

Design by Nicole Savory

figure | 25 |

Design by Dottie Detring

figure | 26 |

Design by Elizabeth Linde (Photograph by Claudia Lopez)

figure |27|

Design by Joseph Wisniewski

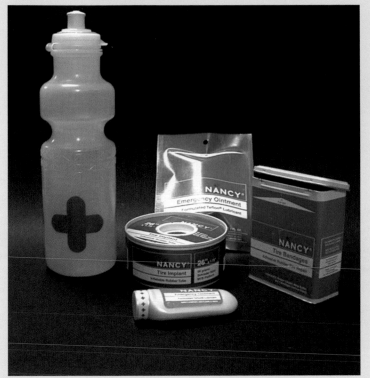

figure |28|

Design by Jason Koebel

figure |29|

© Griffin Chase Oliver, Inc.
(www.griffinchaseoliver.com)

figure |30|

© Studio GT&P (Italy)

figure |31|

© Hornall Anderson Design Works

figure |32|

Packaging Design by Crayon Design & Communication, Montreal, Quebec, Canada (Produced for MSC International)

figure |33|

Packaging Design by Crayon Design & Communication, Montreal, Quebec, Canada (Produced for MSC International)

figure |34|

Design by Jessica Baechle

figure |35|

© Henderson + Aurelio Design Associates, LLC

figure |36|

Design by m-graffik (Croatia)

figure |37|

Design by Diane Benjamin / Pomegranate Design (Photogragh by R. Ascroft)

figure |38|

© CHRW Advertising, LLC

figure |39|

Design by Dmitry Paperny

figure |40|

figure |41|

© Brewer Riddiford, London

figure |42|

© Rob Wright, Redwood Design (South Africa)

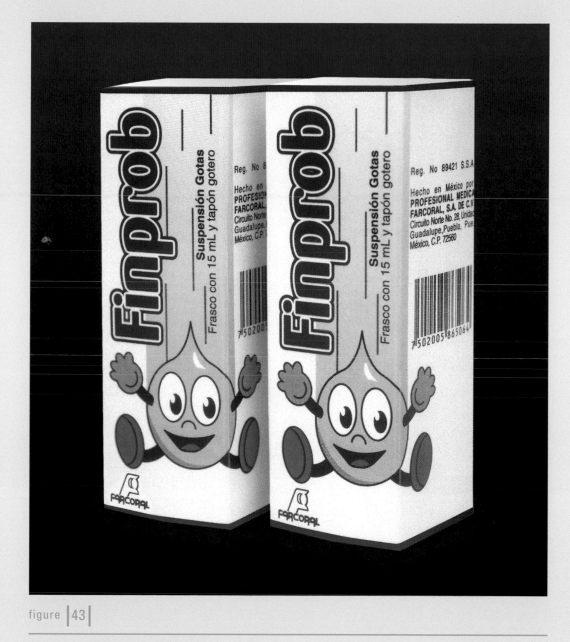

figure |43|

Design by Jose Soto Grageda (Mexico)

figure |44|

© Design by Carol King

figure |45|

Design by Staci Hassan-Fowles (Illustrator: Fiona Godfrey; Photography: Franz Marzouca)

figure |46|

Design by Rei Yoshimoto Wright

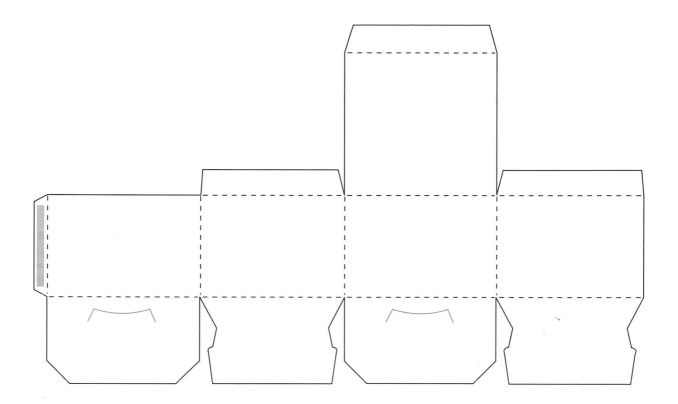

TUCK-LOCK-BOTTOMED BOX

A simple box with minimal gluing. The top closes with a tuck-flap lid, and the bottom employs a multiple tuck-lock system.

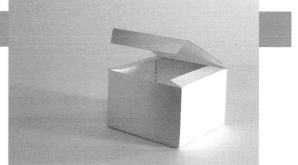

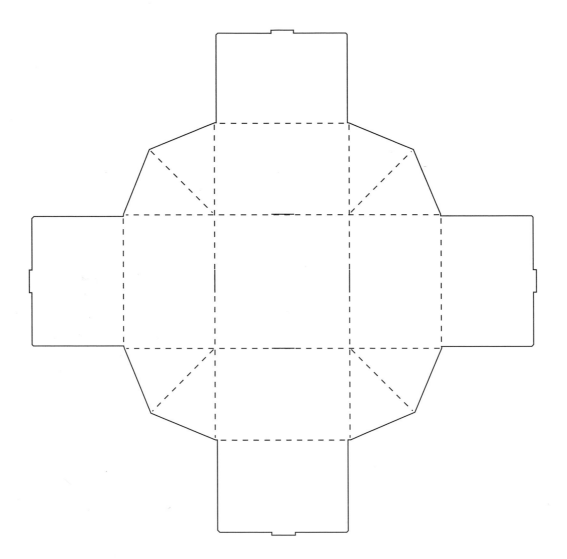

ONE-PIECE OPEN-TOP BOX

An open box that can be assembled
without gluing. Sides fold into cut
locks to stay in place
and add rigidity.

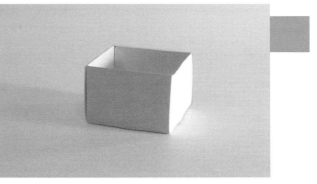

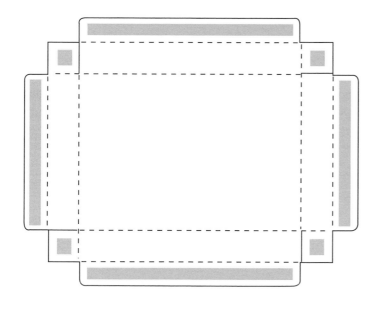

"MATCHBOX" SLIDING TRAY with WRAP

A two-piece box in which a sliding tray is surrounded on four sides by an open-end wraparound. Extra folds and tabs on the tray give it enough strength and rigidity to hold its shape when being pushed and pulled during use.

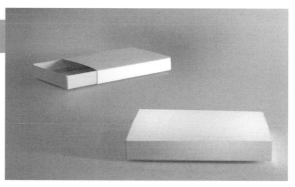

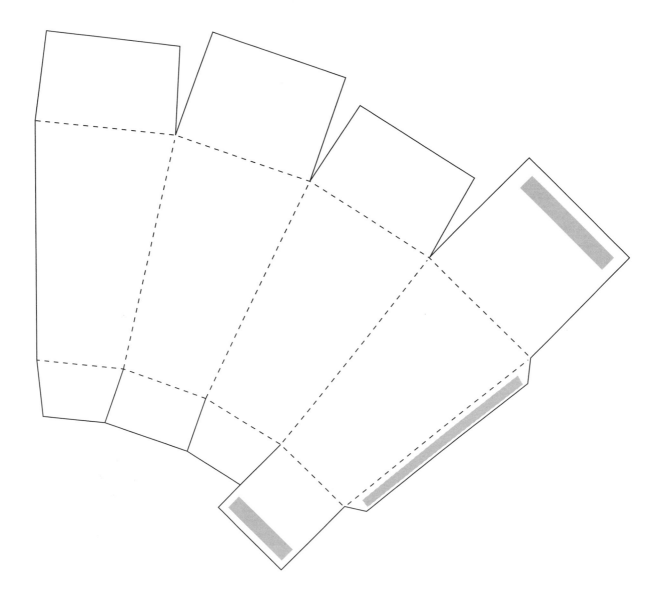

TAPERED-SIDE BOX

A variation of the simple cube. This elegant box can be made by forming base and top from different-size squares.

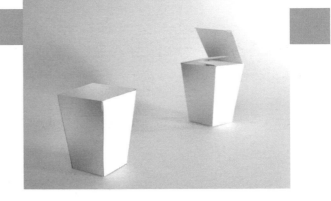

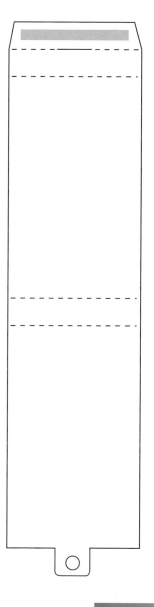

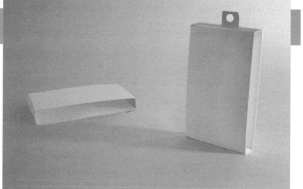

OPEN-SIDED WRAP with HANG TAB

A simple wraparound container with open sides and formed from a single sheet. Tab serves dual purpose of holding wrap together and providing a tab for hook or peg hanging.

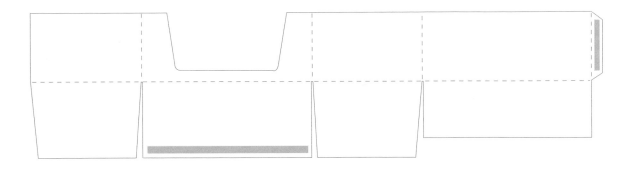

OPEN-FRONT TRAY

A flat tray with full open top and partial front side holds items in place while allowing for easy access to its contents. Works well on a shelf or countertop placement.

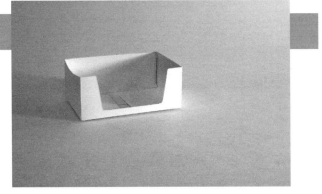

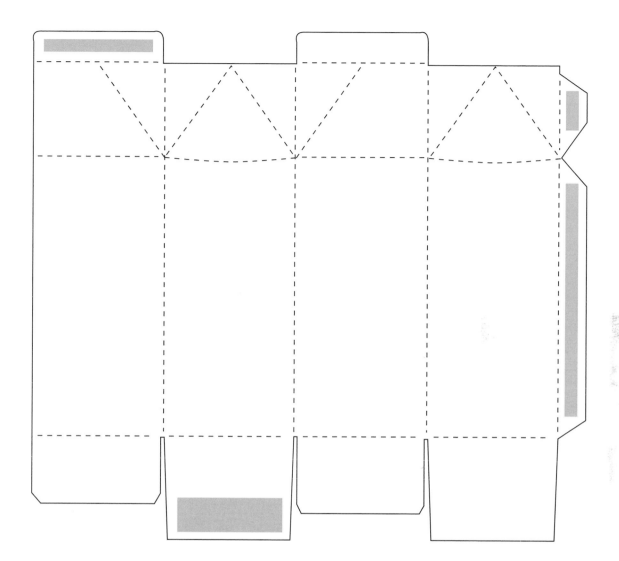

MILK CARTON–STYLE BOX with SPOUT

This familiar form is often used for milk or juices, although it can serve effectively for dry powders as well. Sealed at the top, it features a pour spout that can be opened and closed repeatedly.

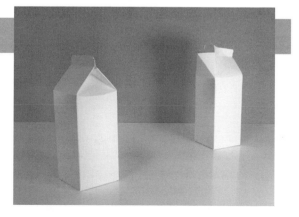

SKEWED or DIAMOND CUBE

Skewing two sides of a cube
to form parallelograms creates this
interesting package structure.

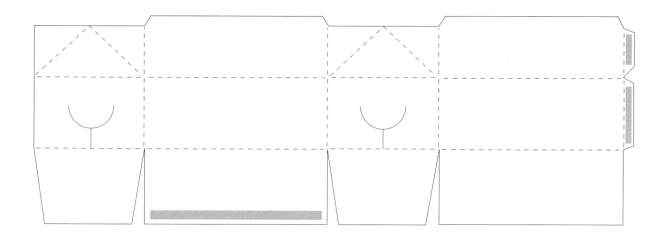

END-TUCK RESEALABLE BOX

This form has an attached lid that folds in and down to create two tucks for the rounded end slots.

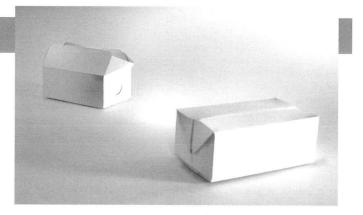

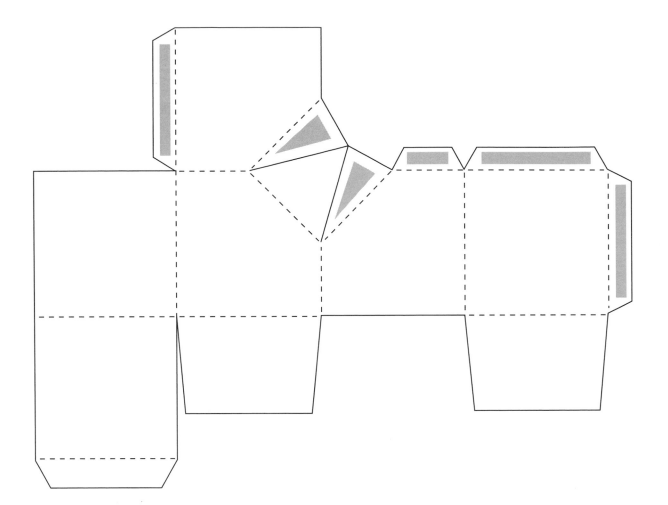

CORNER-FACET SEVEN-SIDED BOX

A basic cube with a "cutaway" corner.

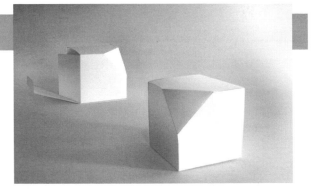

PYRAMIDS

A popular polyhedron form, the pyramid, is a strong, rigid package structure. The pyramid is evocative and mysterious, reminiscent of the monuments of ancient Egypt, a prism, or rays of light breaking through a cloud. With its sides meeting at a common vertex and having a flat, wide base, the pyramid is also a particularly stable form.

EQUAL-SIDED FOUR-PANEL PYRAMID

A tetrahedron formed from four equilateral triangles. This structure can be oriented in several different ways for interesting design possibilities.

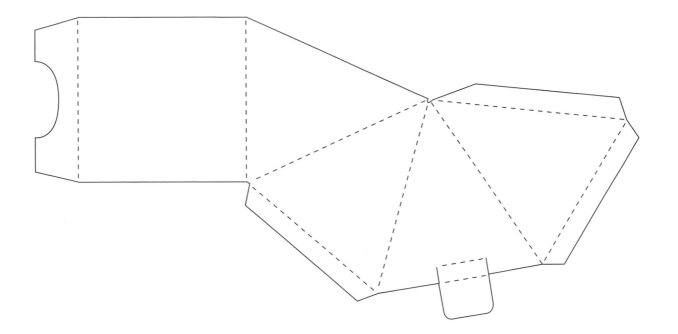

TUCK-LOCK PYRAMID with BASE

Four-sided pyramid on a square base. Tuck-lock closure has this form opening by folding back the top four panels.

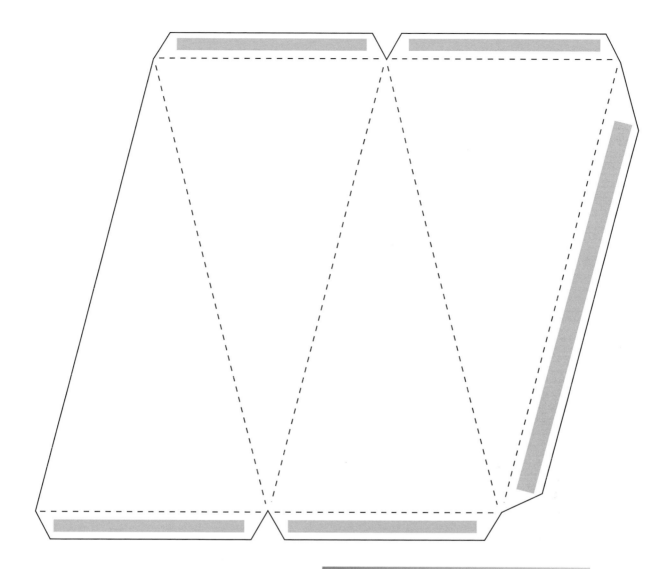

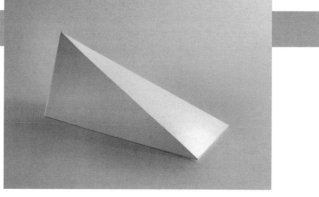

ELONGATED TETRAHEDRON

A four-sided pyramid with elongated, sloping sides.

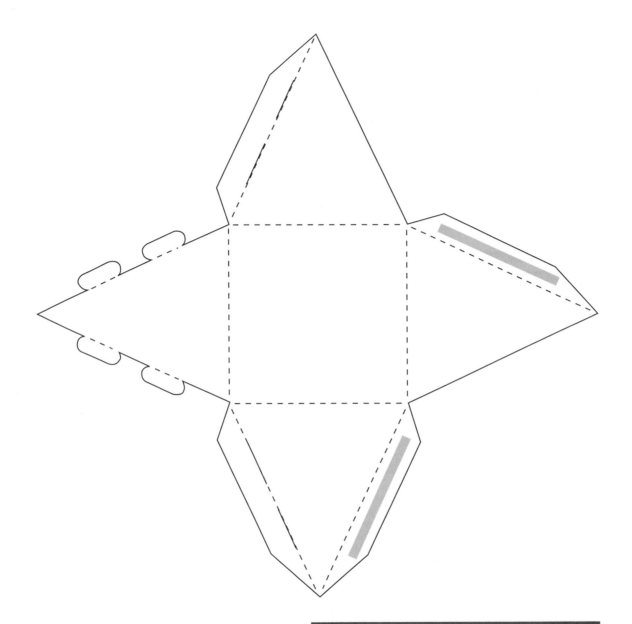

FRONT-TAB OPEN PYRAMID

This pyramid-shaped form has a
front side that folds down to open,
and closes with tab-and-slit closures.
Only two glue panels keep this
pyramid together.

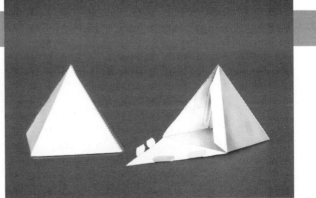

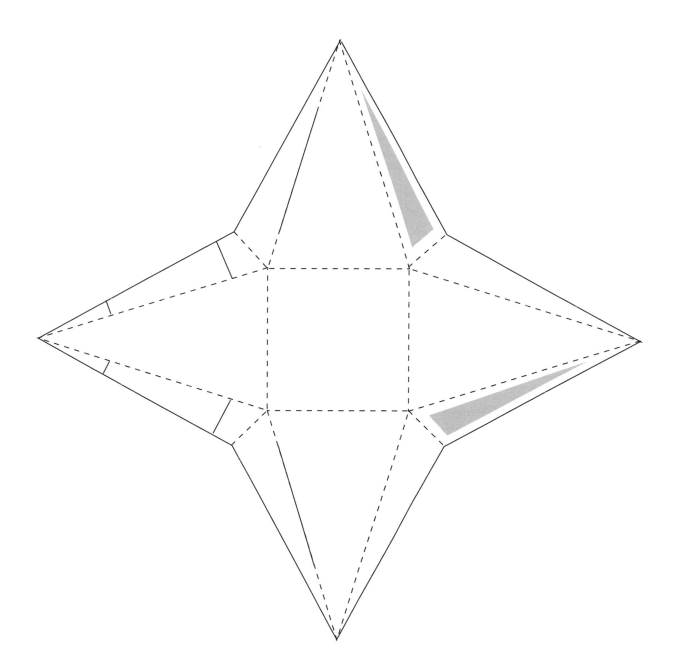

ACCORDION-FOLD PYRAMID

Four-sided pyramid on a square base. Tuck-lock closure has this form opening by folding back one side.

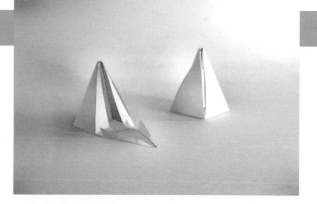

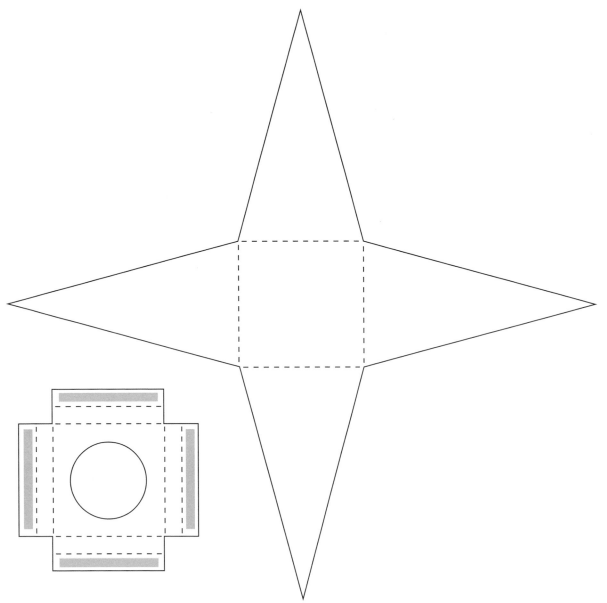

PRESENTATION PYRAMID

This form features a presentation base inside the pyramid and a closure made from a Chinese coin.

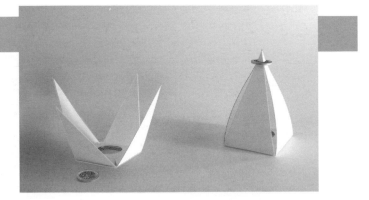

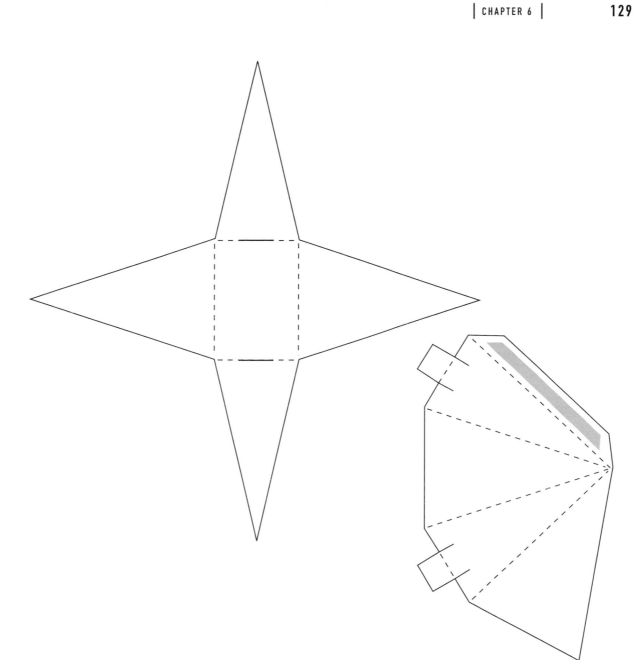

SLIP-TOP PYRAMID with TUCK LOCKS

A two-piece form.
The outer pyramid slips off to reveal
the inner form, with sides that fold
down like flower petals.

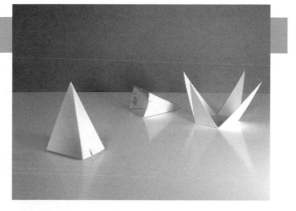

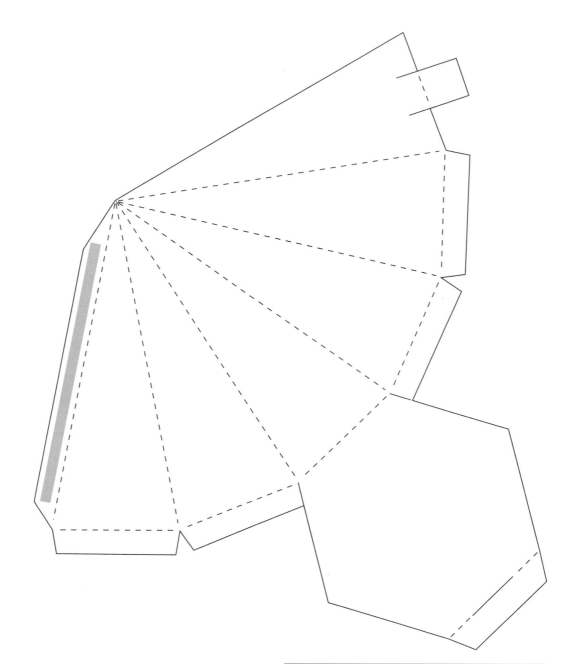

HEXAGON-BASED PYRAMID

A pyramid with six sides and a hexagon base. Tuck-lock closure along base allows this form to be opened and closed.

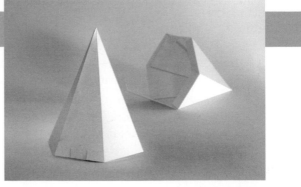

CYLINDERS AND CONES

Cylinders can be found in many examples of packaging. A number of cylindrical packages take the form of metal cans, but can be found in paperboard packaging as well. Powders such as salt, oatmeal, and carpet freshener lend themselves particularly well to the cylinder paperboard container. If you were to take a flimsy drinking straw, stand it on end, and push straight down with your finger on the top end, you would see how rigid a structure the cylinder is.

When determining the length of the side to wrap around the circular base, designers employ the geometry formula for finding a circle's circumference:

C (circumference) = pi (3.14) $\times$ D (diameter of the circle).

For example, a cylinder with a circular base of 4" (its diameter), multiplied by 3.14, will give a circumference of 12.56". Therefore, the side will need to be at least 12.56" to completely wrap around the 4" base—a bit more for an overlap.

The cone has a triangular profile much like a pyramid, but where the pyramid is made up of several flat sides, the cone has only one rounded side sitting on a flat base.

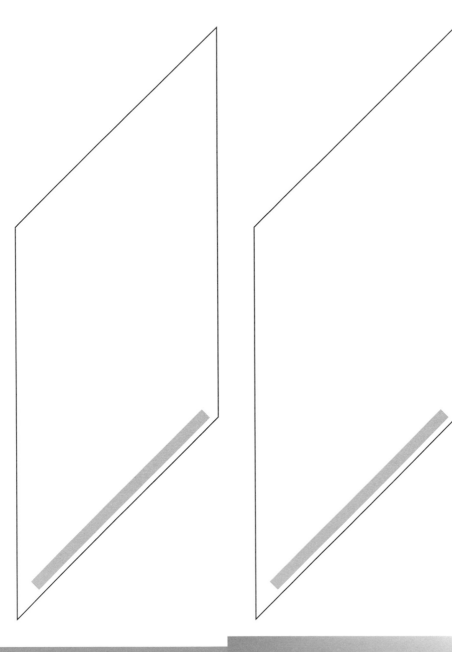

SPIRAL-WRAP CYLINDRICAL TUBE

A two-piece cylindrical tube. Trapezoid is wrapped into tube of the desired diameter and glued along one edge. A second piece is aligned with the ending edge of the first and wrapped again to hold the shape.

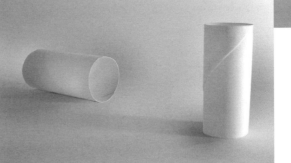

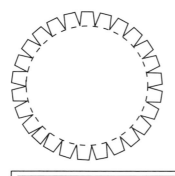

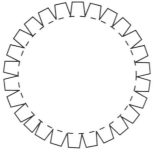

LIDDED CYLINDER

A simple cylinder with separate lid.

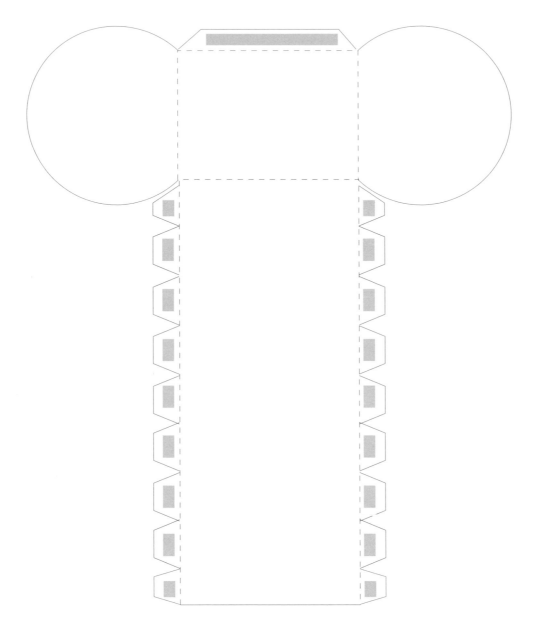

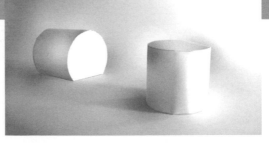

SEMICYLINDER

A cylinder with a flat side.
The additional plane enables this
package to either lay flat or
stand on end.

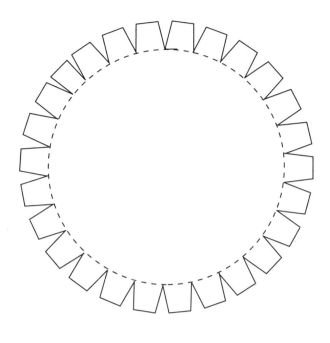

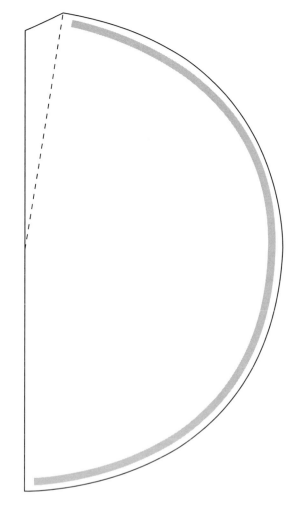

SIMPLE CONE with BASE

This basic cone is a simple, elegant shape that's easy to make. The large, flat base makes this a very stable structure with a great deal of side strength.

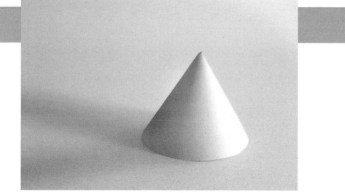

NOTE:
*Glue tab is not scored,
as this would encourage
the cone to angle at the
junction point instead of
continuing the curve.*

TRUNCATED CONE

**A truncated cone with
parallel top and base.**

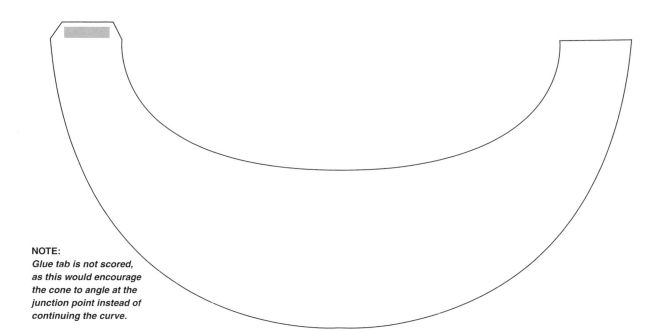

NOTE:
*Glue tab is not scored,
as this would encourage
the cone to angle at the
junction point instead of
continuing the curve.*

OBLIQUE TRUNCATED CONE

**A truncated cone with its
top at an angle to the base.**

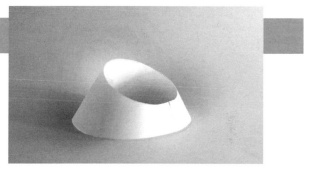

UNUSUAL SHAPES

Of course, some boxes don't fall into any of the neat categories of the four basic shapes. These are the rule breakers—the model patterns that leave you thinking "I wonder how?"

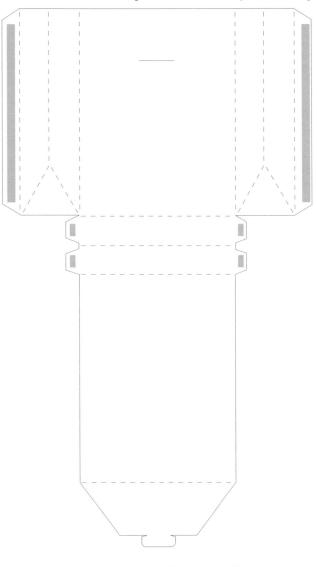

STANDING ENVELOPE with FLAP

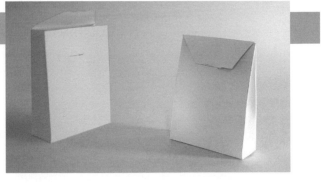

This tent-sided envelope has a flat base for standing upright and fold-over flap that secures with a tuck.

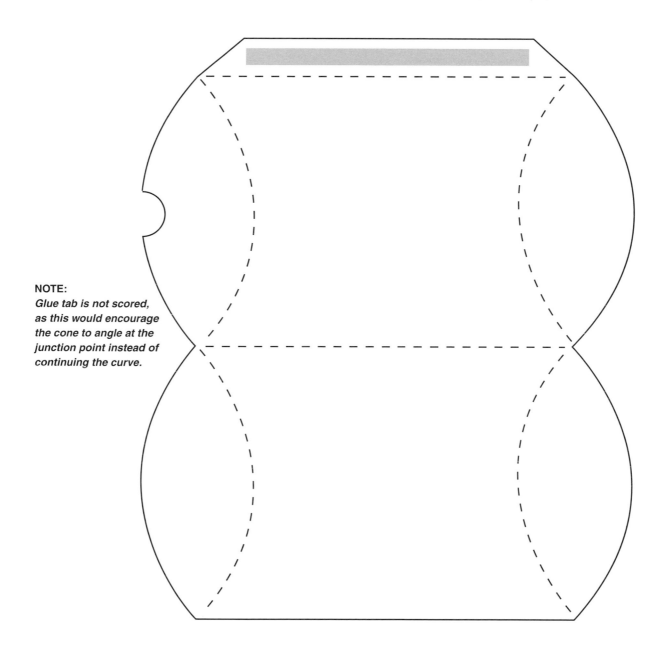

NOTE:
*Glue tab is not scored,
as this would encourage
the cone to angle at the
junction point instead of
continuing the curve.*

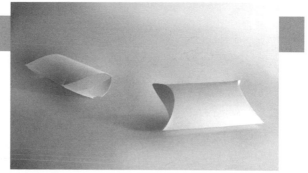

PILLOW-PACK BOX

A very simple structure. Curved
score lines fold in to puff the box
into the shape of a pillow. The tension
of the scores holds the
end flaps in place.

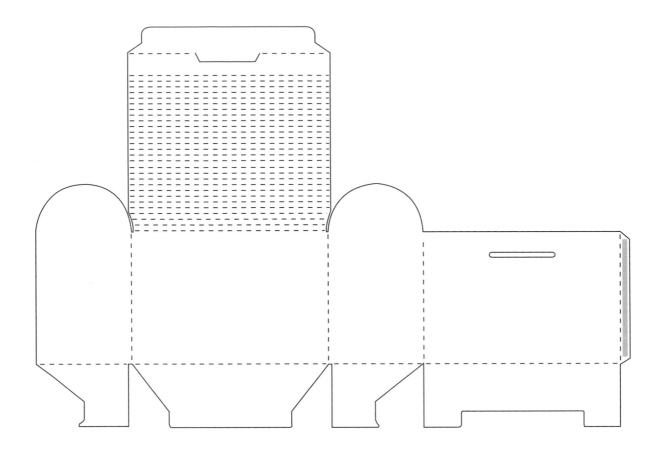

"LUNCH PAIL" ROUND-TOP BOX

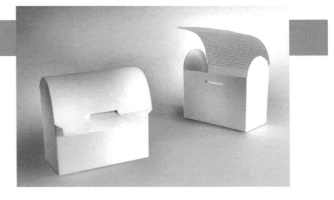

This box has rounded side panels to guide the lid into its curve. A tuck lock secures the lid and the interlocking tab system holds the base of the box together. Bristol board will bend freely, but heavier stock may need additional scoring along the lines shown.

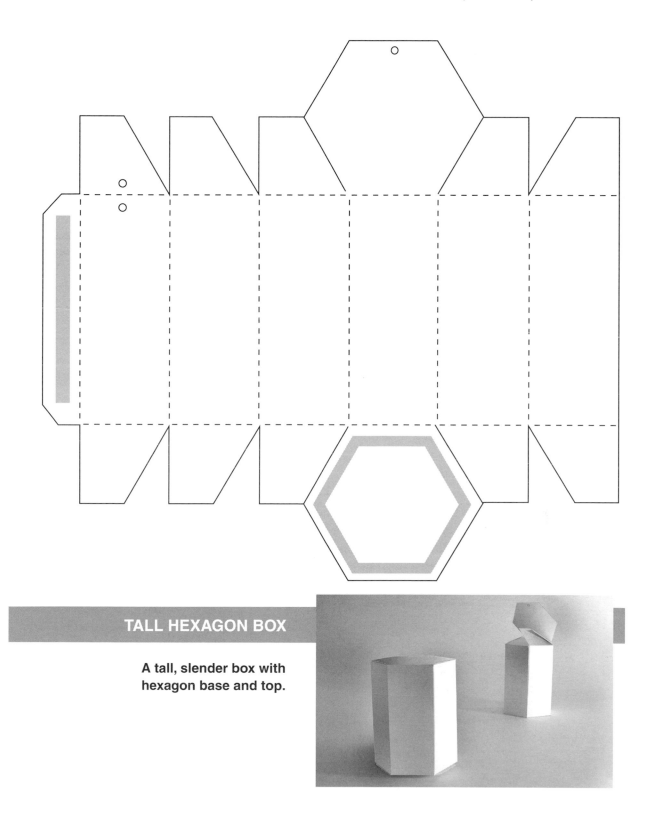

TALL HEXAGON BOX

A tall, slender box with
hexagon base and top.

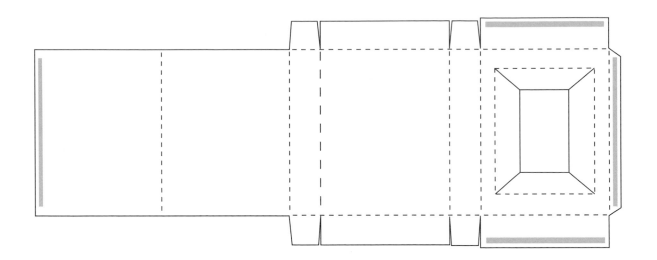

DIMENSIONAL FRAME with COVER

This box creates a framed receptacle for protection and display. The double-thick attached cover adds to the presentation.

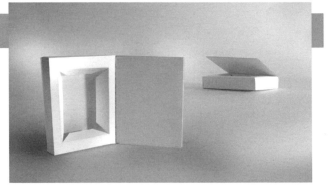

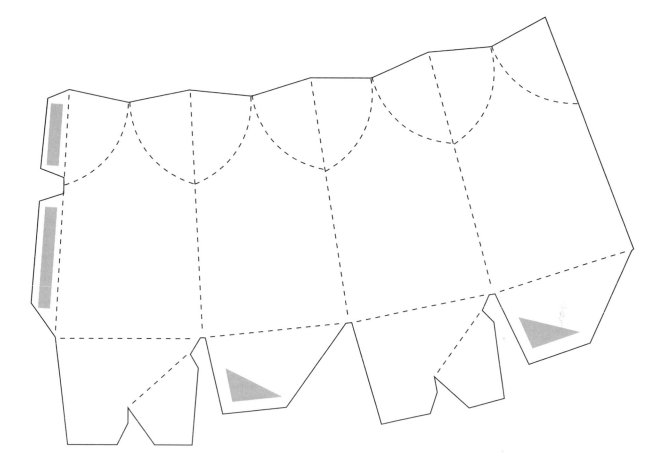

"FLOWER TOP" SCORED BOX

The curved scores enable the four
top panels to be folded inward for
this decorative closure.

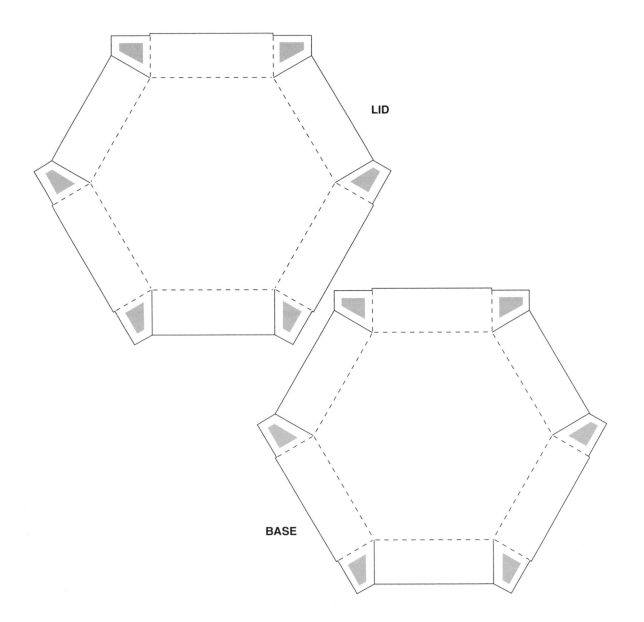

LID

BASE

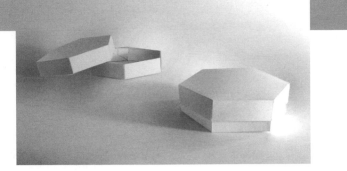

TWO-PIECE HEXAGON BOX

Two hexagons—one slightly larger
than the other—create this box
with removable lid.

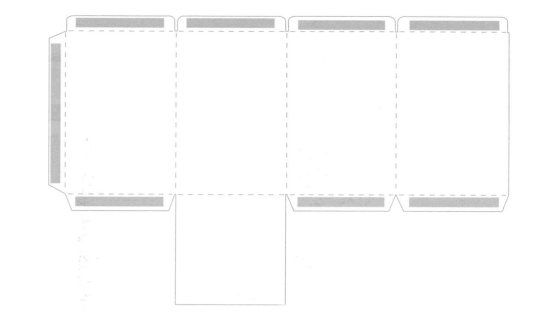

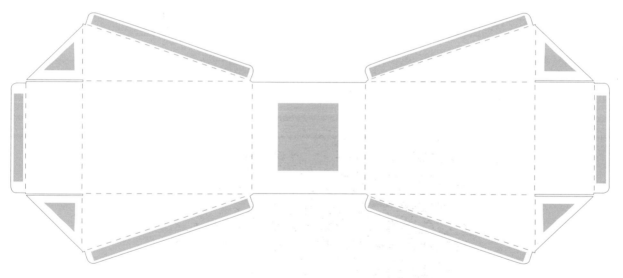

TWO-PIECE WING-SIDED BOX

This box, made from two separate pieces joined at the bottom, has an interesting and interactive closure. The two wing panels fold down to reveal the open-top box.

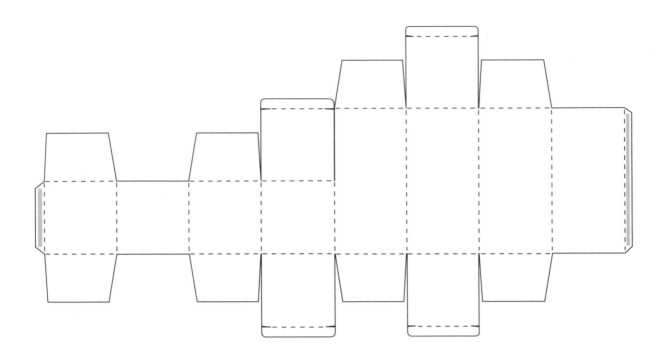

TWO-TIERED SECTIONAL BOX

Two attached boxes with a shared edge add movement and scale to this package form.

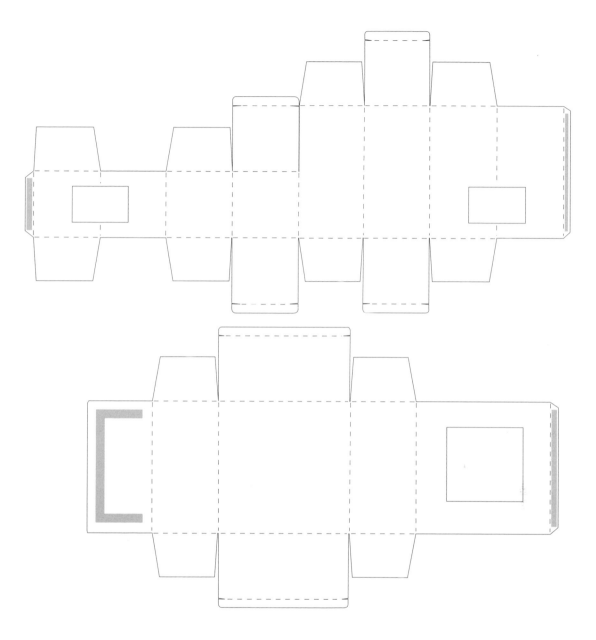

TIERED SECTIONAL BOX with DIE CUT

A unique form of three attached
boxes that fold into a $\frac{7}{8}$ cube.
Here, a series of three die-cut
windows display box interiors.

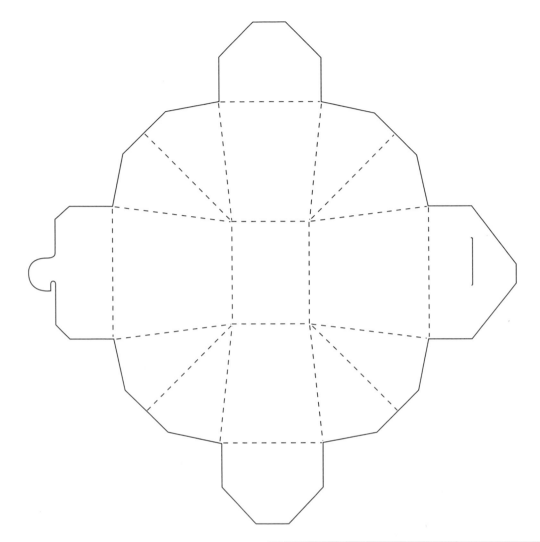

"TAKE-OUT"-STYLE ANGLED-WALL BOX

The one-piece construction of this box forms a strong, sealed pocket. If plastic-coated paperboard is used, this box will hold liquids. Shown here with a wire hanger to hold form together at two points.

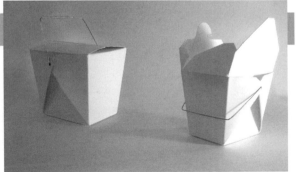

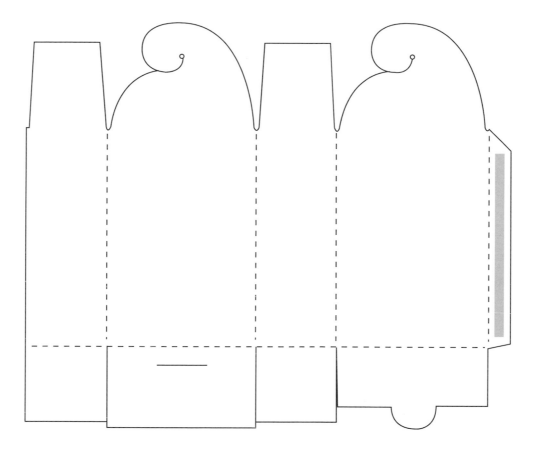

INTERLOCK-TAB-TOP BOX

A semisealed box with nonscored top panels held in place by interlocking cuts. The decorative interlocks may be shaped in any number of ways for creative effect.

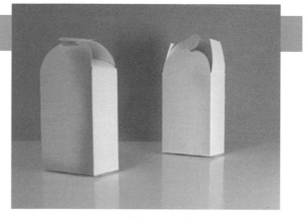

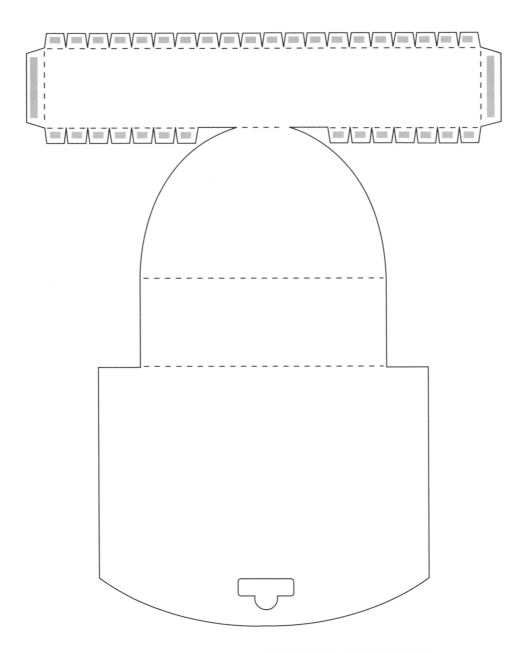

HALF-CYLINDER with BACK

A display box that can either hang on a peg or sit on a shelf. The half-cylinder provides dimension while the large flat backer is an excellent surface for graphics and text.

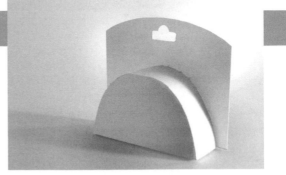

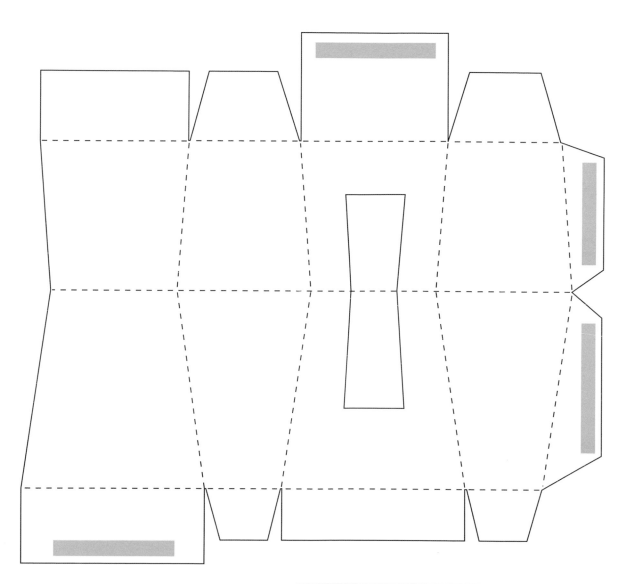

SCORED ANGLE-SIDED BOX

Creative scoring can yield new shapes. Example shown here features a die-cut window.

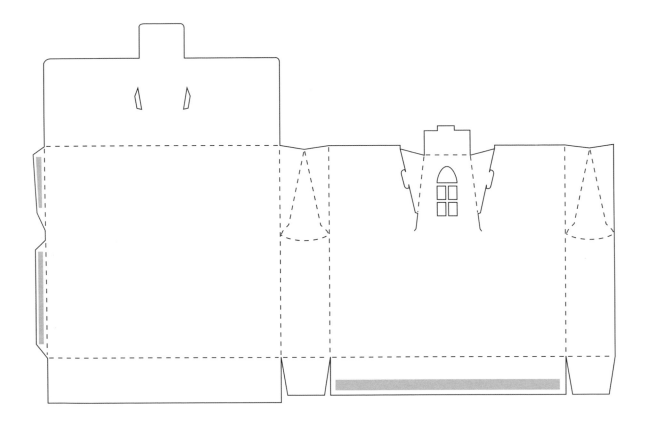

VICTORIAN-STYLE HOUSE with GABLE

A stylish box in the shape of a Victorian building. The protruding gable and die-cut five-pane window add to the effect while serving as the package closure.

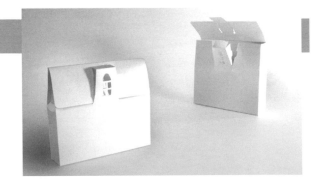

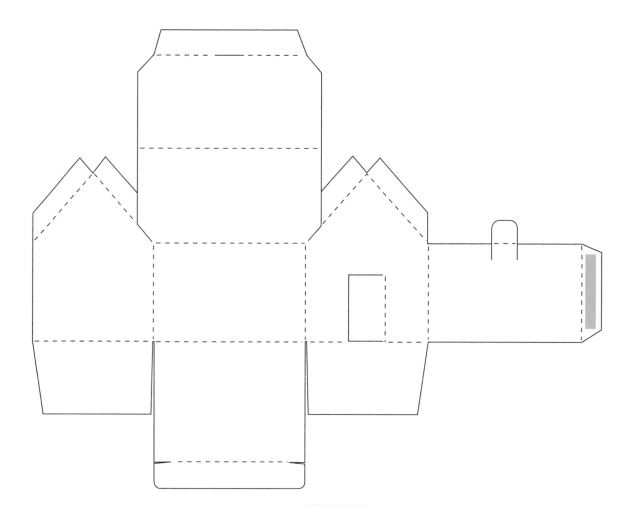

COTTAGE-SHAPED BOX with TUCK LOCK

A playful box in the shape of a house
with a raising roof lid.

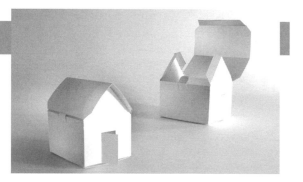

PROFILE

Daryl Woods

Daryl Woods founded Public Image Design in 1985. Since then, the Toronto-based graphic design and advertising consultancy has grown to include clients from as far away as Australia and Europe. "Public Image Design is a small firm," Woods says. "The majority of our packaging work comes through marketing agencies representing international clients in our national market. The assignments I've handled range from industrial auto parts to wine and liquor packaging—the latter being the focus of our attention today."

Woods describes his role as a designer as one of looking into a mirror: "To be a good packaging designer, you need to be able to think like the consumer. A great piece of design can be a com-

mercial failure if it doesn't appeal to the target consumer. One of the things I enjoy about much of my work is that I am part of the target market I'm designing for. That kind of thing is invaluable; some of my clients are far too close to their industries, and though they produce great products, they find it difficult to be objective about marketing.

"Open your eyes. Explore all types of packaging and analyze what you find attractive. Don't seek to copy it—just learn to recognize the elements of

SUMMING IT UP

Robert Gair and his folding cardboard box paved the way for more and more inventive and elaborate packaging. Today, countless shapes of cardboard containers are not only possible, but almost omnipresent. Through careful consideration of the product to be packed and a study of basic forms that can be elaborated upon and modified, the designer can understand and produce inventive and creative package forms and accurate design templates.

With one of Public Image's clients, an Italian winery producing vino novello, the strength of the packaging not only influences sales and perception of the product—it determines whether it will be imported to Canada at all. "The market is controlled by a government agency. The agency chooses a limited number of 'Nouveau-style' wines for distribution and sale each year. Many competitors make submissions to the agency to be chosen by the supplier. There are a small number of categories—most are French, and only one comes from Italy. At the time the selection is made—early September—the wine is still grape on the vine. The choice is based on packaging and marketing plans. If the product we design for isn't chosen, that work will never be produced. We've been successful for five consecutive years in securing the selection and order for our client—getting an order is like winning a sweepstakes."

Unlike other wines, Nouveau wines are seasonal, meaning they are produced, sold, and consumed within a few months' time. Woods looks at the rel-

© Public Image Design

atively tight design deadlines and short product life as an opportunity. "One of the interesting things about this assignment, from a strategic perspective, is that the product has a very short selling period—just six weeks. This allows us to be much bolder and trendier with design than if the product was to have years of shelf presence."

You can visit Public Image Design on the Internet at www.publicimagedesign.com ■

Design by Dottie Detring

Figure |6-5|

Don't forget that these patterns can be applied to materials other than paperboard. This designer formed boxes from stiff acetate.

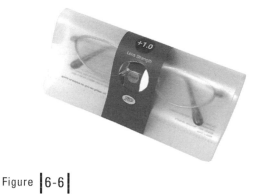

© AM Associates

Figure |6-6|

AM Associates used frosted plastic to add visibility and a touch of mystery to this package.

in review

1. What were the advantages of the folding cardboard box?

2. What are some considerations a designer must keep in mind when determining a package's structure?

3. Why might it be wise to explore several options for constructing the same basic form?

exercises

1. Find four different rectangular boxes. Carefully disassemble them and draw a template for each. Make a note of each difference in their layouts and explain a reason for the variation.

2. Construct at least two 3-D models from each of the four sections of patterns in this chapter. Choosing one from each section, modify the pattern by altering its dimensions, orientation of panels, or how it opens. What changes occurred? Were there any problems with your new template you didn't foresee?

3. Reproduce these sixty patterns and arrange them in a ring binder. As you modify these existing patterns or create new ones of your own, add them to the binder. These will be an excellent resource.

CHAPTER

7

"Everyone lives by selling something."

Robert Louis Stevenson

Chapter Objectives

Provide an overview of point-of-purchase displays

Determine the venues for point-of-sale marketing

Explore a series of patterns for point-of-purchase displays

Introduction

A paramount objective in the field of retail package design is to get your package noticed. Forget the "fifteen minutes of fame"; if your package garners fifteen *seconds* of your audience's attention, it is well on its way to success. With the myriad of competitors fighting for eye time and shelf space, a package's life and death depends upon those few moments of a consumer's interest while walking down a store aisle.

One of the most effective ways of grabbing that attention is through the point-of-purchase display. A point-of-purchase display—referred to as a P.O.P.—attracts the audience, draws them in close, and does its darnedest to make a sale.

THE SALE BEGINS WITH EYE CONTACT

The study of Gestalt teaches that objects of similar size or shape tend to be grouped together and perceived as a mass. But the whole point of successful package design is to stand out from the crowd—often a difficult thing to do when packages are

figure | 7-1 |

A simple and effective counter-top display.

figure | 7-2 |

Store shelves are filled with packages, each fighting for attention.

| SURVEY |

In 1965, the Swiss designer and educator Armin Hofmann stated: "We must accustom ourselves to the idea that our mental and vocational equipment must be constantly refurbished."

Continuous education remains a priority for designers today.

I agree strongly.	**92%**
I agree somewhat.	**6%**
I disagree.	**5%**

Totals shown may be more or less than 100% due to rounding.

SOURCE: The International Council of Graphic Design Associations

figure | 7-3 |

Shelf talkers are simple, inexpensive, and surprisingly effective.

displayed side by side with other analogous products. A well-designed point-of-purchase display can help separate a product from its competitors, focus consumer attention, and serve as a directed advertisement, targeting the shopper at the exact moment of sale.

How does a P.O.P. work? The display can be placed in a variety of locations, either directly on the shelf among the other packaging, in a place within the aisle, on the "end cap" (the shelf formed at the end of an aisle), or even at the checkout counter. These displays are usually colorful, dynamic, and eye-catching, drawing the consumer's attention to a specific product and, equally important, away from rival products.

TYPES OF P.O.P.S

Displays can take many forms. Simple "shelf talkers" and "danglers"—cards that hang from a shelf or the ceiling—can advertise sales, product improvements, or new items. Despite their size, these small displays are remarkably effective selling tools.

End caps or end-aisle displays are larger displays placed at the end of a shopping aisle, just as the name suggests. These displays are successful for several reasons. They attractively display packaging; their placement at the end of the aisle gets them noticed by customers who were not otherwise planning to shop for the product; they physically separate the package from the competitors, greatly reducing the fight for interest in other packages.

Floor stands are the largest of the point-of-purchase displays. Situated either in the aisle where the product is normally stocked or in another part of the store altogether, the size of the floor stand ensures that the package is seen. Floor stands can be large cardboard advertisements, or may actually hold and display the packaging on shelves, bins, or hooks. Floor stands are often made from corrugated cardboard or form board and printed with striking graphics, although some floor stands serve as permanent kiosks for the products. Interactive CD displays and touch-screen displays are examples of these, and may be constructed of wood, metal, acrylic, or other substantial and durable material.

Another common P.O.P. is the countertop display, because it can be located on a shelf, an end cap, counter, or even right beside the checkout cash register. These P.O.P.s play upon the "last-minute" aspect of shopping. How many times have you gone to a store for one item and left with several? Chances are, walking down an aisle or waiting in line to check out, your eye fell upon a product that made you think, "Well, as long as I'm here . . ." or "Oh, I forgot I need . . ." And chances also are that many of these extra purchases were found at point-of-purchase displays.

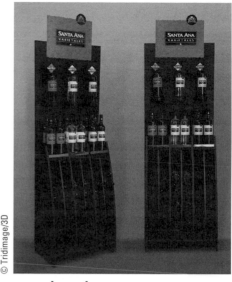

© Tridimage/3D

figure | 7-4 |

These wine displays are sturdy enough to hold the weight of their product, and can be used for a long period of time, making the expense of materials worthwhile.

THE IMPULSIVE BUYER

P.O.P. displays have developed into one of the most valuable tools in marketing. As the shopping experience becomes increasingly self-service, consumers are more and more influenced by the selling power of in-store displays. Research has indicated that up to 25 percent of our purchases are "impulse buys"—products

© Griffin Chase Oliver, Inc. / www.griffinchaseoliver.com

figure | 7-5 |

Countertop displays are versatile and can be placed on shelves, counters, or near the cashier station.

© Design by Jason Koebel

figure | 7-6 |

This countertop P.O.P. makes creative use of photography and materials to promote a disc of computer fonts.

| SURVEY |

How do you calculate your prices?

By calculating my expenses
and my hourly rate **59%**

By comparing what my
colleagues charge and then
making an estimate **29%**

According to a price list
provided by my design
association **14%**

Totals shown may be more or less than 100% due to rounding.

SOURCE: The International Council of Graphic Design Associations

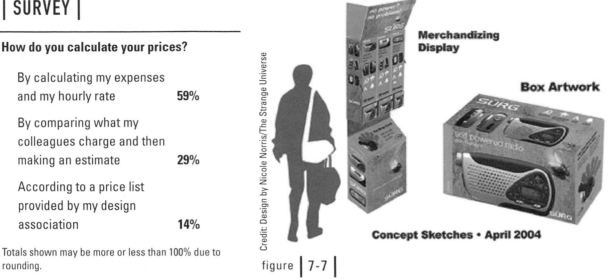

Credit: Design by Nicole Norris/The Strange Universe

Merchandizing Display

Box Artwork

Concept Sketches • April 2004

figure | 7-7 |

A human silhouette is used to design this P.O.P. concept sketch in proper scale.

that we had no intention of buying when entering the store, but decided upon once there. Moving through a market or store, the shopper is enticed by a well-designed display, even if the product featured is not on the shopping list. By placing a package where its message is most effective—in front of the consumer precisely when purchases are being made—P.O.P. displays become effective, targeted designs.

DESIGNING FOR DISPLAY

Much like packaging itself, the art of P.O.P. design is part packaging, part structural engineering, part advertising, and part psychology; Except that creating a compelling P.O.P. must take into account these additional factors:

Credit: Mark Weisz Design

figure | 7-8 |

Box becomes display for this carton of Ladybug chocolates.

- *The P.O.P. display should complement and augment the current advertising campaign for the product.*

- *It must be designed to show the package in its best light.*

- *If the display is to be short-lived (a two- to three-week in-store run, as is the case with most P.O.P.s), it should reinforce an in-progress promotion, sale, rebate, or other time-sensitive event.*

- *The display must be able to ship preassembled or easy-to-assemble on site, with instructions.*

Each P.O.P. should follow these goals if it is to justify the added printing, material, and labor expenses of producing an in-store display.

WHERE SHOULD A P.O.P. BE PLACED?

When looking to place a point-of-purchase display, it's best to evaluate and prioritize the goals of the presentation. Is this a display to introduce a new product? If so, it may be wise to place it near other, more established, products that are similar to lure consumers away from products they are accustomed to finding in a particular part of the store. Is the display intended to reinforce a current advertising campaign or promotion that doesn't necessarily reflect a drop in price? In that case, an end-cap or end-aisle display may be more appropriate. Why? Again, consumers who may not have come to shop for that particular item may see the display, remember the ads they've viewed in other media, and connect to the product. Additionally, end-cap displays remove the package from competitors, making price comparison difficult and reducing the impact of competing packaging.

The goals of any marketing or display campaign are complex and varied. Each point-of-purchase display should be able to answer the identified goals in tone, character, structure, and placement.

These goals impact decisions when choosing the material from which the display should be made. Disposable materials such as corrugated cardboard, foam board, or extruded corrugated plastic are suitable for time-sensitive promotions or sales that coincide with specific advertising campaigns because they can serve their purpose cheaply and then be discarded. Each of these materials is strong, lightweight, ships and assembles easily, and offers highly printable surfaces. Permanent displays can be constructed from other, less ephemeral, materials like acrylic, wood, or metal, since they should be expected to hold up to greater use and maintain their appearance for a longer period of time.

POINT-OF-PURCHASE DISPLAY PATTERNS

The following pages contain a small sampling of various P.O.P. display patterns. As is true with the packaging patterns in Chapter 6, there are literally countless forms, each with many variations and possibilities for creating displays. These are meant to serve as starting points in your own studies of point-of-purchase design.

| TIPS |

Although it may seem that impulse buying is random and unexpected, the designer should be aware that a great deal of science, psychology, and marketing research focuses on the subject. For instance, studies have shown that most people enter a store and turn immediately to the right. The placement of expensive items or P.O.P. displays just inside and to the right lures customers to make large purchases first. Smaller items or discounted merchandise is often placed deeper into the sales floor or near the check-out registers when shoppers subconsciously know they have less money left after the bigger purchases.

© Studio GT&P

figure | 7-9 |

A P.O.P. can be designed to ship, dispense, and promote a product, all at once.

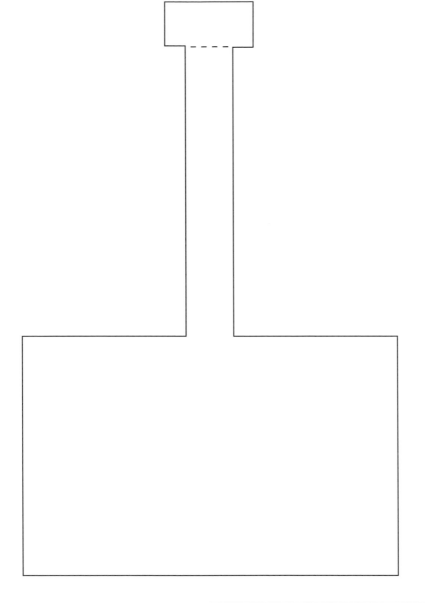

SHELF-TALKER P.O.P.

This simple and easy to construct P.O.P. hangs from the shelf above a selected item, calling attention and advertising a discount, special promotion, or other feature.

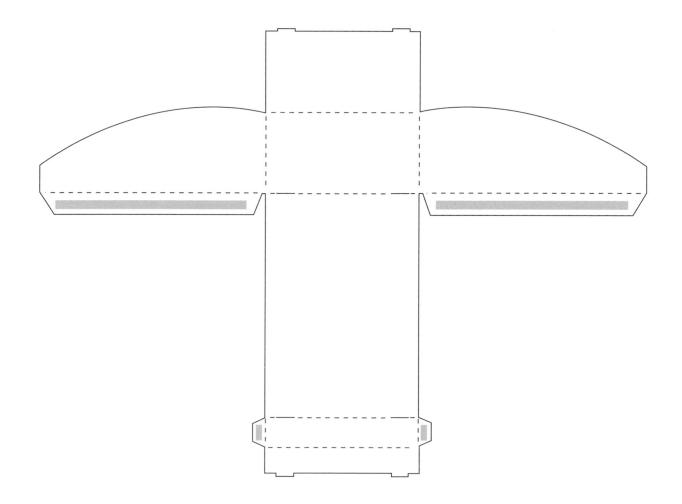

ARCHED-SIDED COUNTERTOP P.O.P.

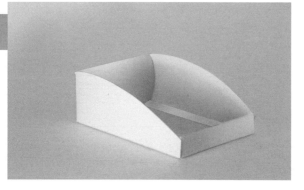

This is a simple variation of the open-tray box, but larger and usually made of a more dense substrate. An effective display of small, last-minute items displayed on a counter-top, often near the checkout.

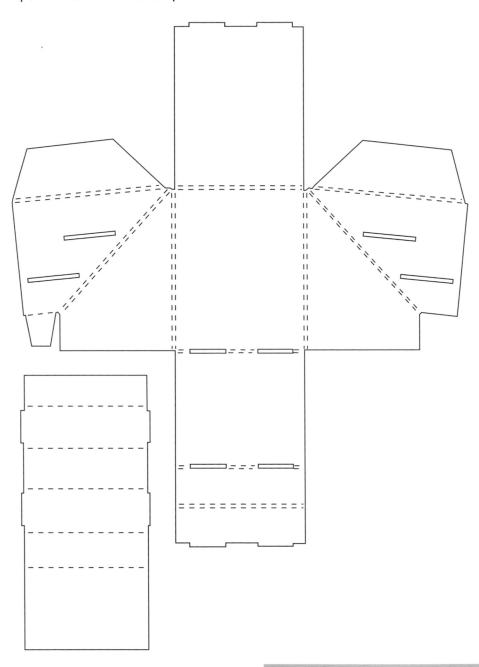

TIER-SHELVED P.O.P.

A sturdy, free-standing P.O.P., this can be constructed as a countertop display or enlarged into a floor-standing P.O.P. The tiered shelves allow for visibility of displayed products.

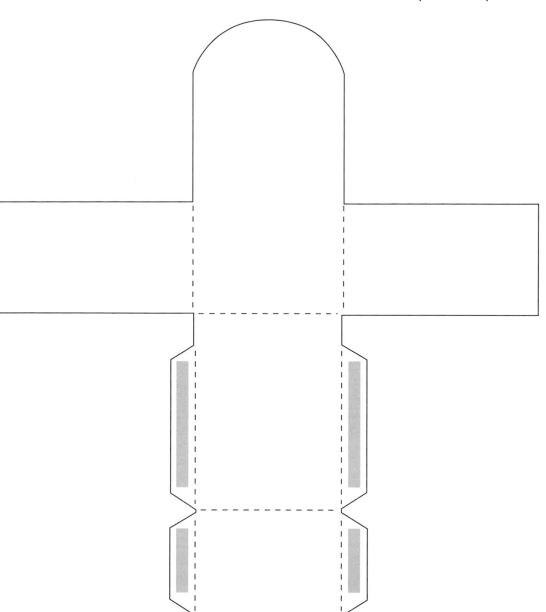

HIGH-BACK COUNTERTOP P.O.P.

The high back on this P.O.P. is perfect for graphics, typography, or images to direct the audience toward the featured item.

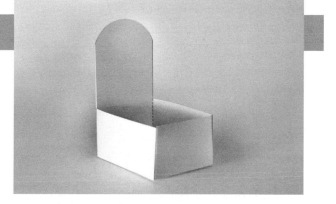

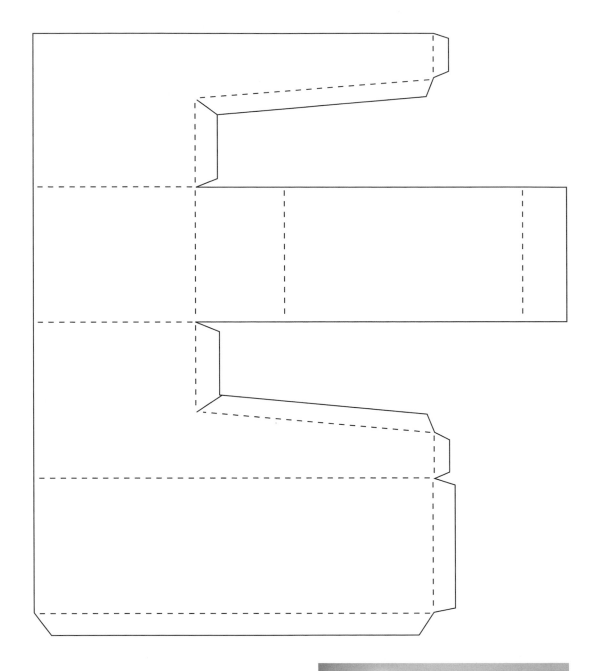

TALL-BACK FLOOR-STANDING P.O.P.

A tall-backed P.O.P. for displaying large items or a series of smaller items, if the back is fitted with hooks, pegs or shelves. This floor display may be placed in an aisle or anywhere in the store.

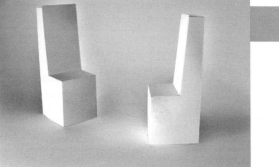

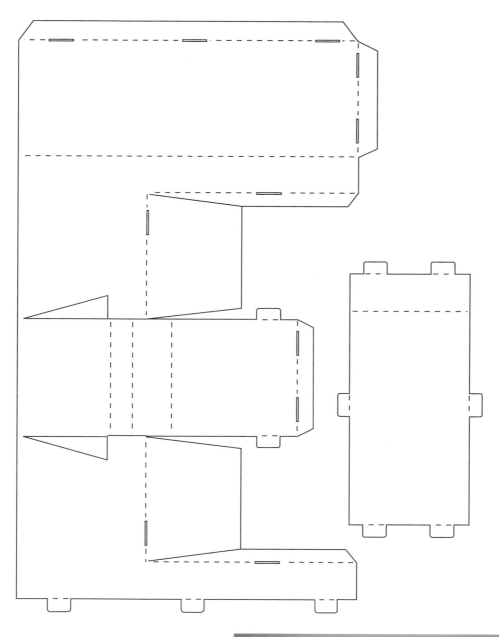

NOTCHED-FRONT FLOOR P.O.P.

A more distinctive variation of the tall-back floor-standing P.O.P., this display may feature a single item or may be modified to show off multiple products in the same way as the tall-back.

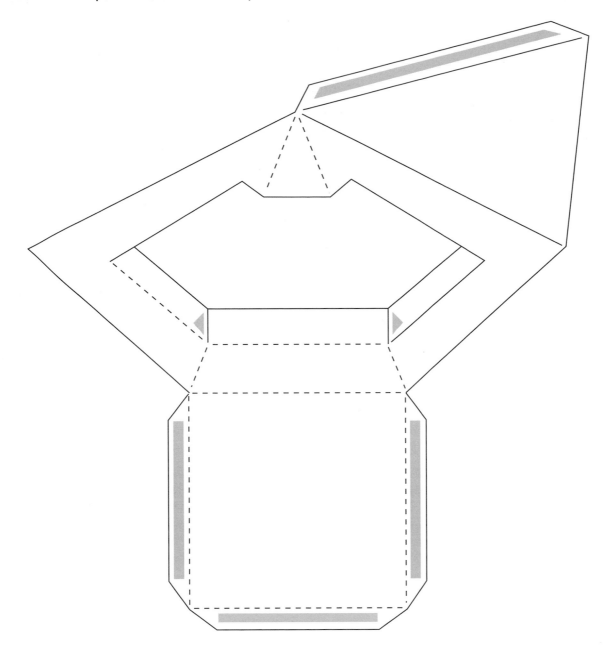

OPEN-FRONT PYRAMID P.O.P.

A four-sided pyramid form wih an
open front for product display.
Attention-getting shape offests the
fact that it normally cannot hold a lot
of product, and must be refilled often.

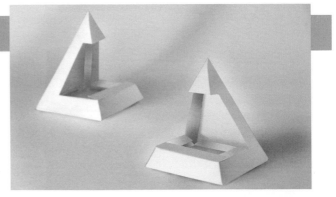

figure | 7-10 |

Burt's Bees uses this point-of-purchase display to place the product—in this case, a lip balm—at the checkout counter to draw last-minute sales.

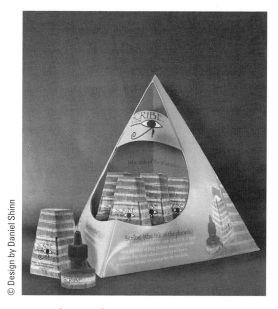

figure | 7-11 |

A pyramid display references the shape of these individual packages of writing and drawing ink, and seeks to connect the product with the ancient Egyptian birth of writing and history.

SUMMING IT UP

In this chapter, you've read about the power of the point-of-purchase display. As a product is introduced to the public, many aspects beyond the package design come into play to determine its success. There is the product's concept and production, of course, the package design, transportation and distribution concerns, advertising in any and all appropriate media (print, television, radio, billboards, and the Web)—all working, ideally, in harmony to speak to the quality, spirit, and particular attributes of the product to get the message out. Not the least of considerations, the point-of-purchase display is an effective and important culmination of all these efforts—it represents the final push, the so-called last three feet of marketing the product, and is one of the only pieces of the campaign that comes into play when product, consumer, opportunity, intent, and money all come together at the same place and time. A good designer will understand and appreciate the P.O.P. and use it to its best advantage.

review questions

1. What does the acronym P.O.P. stand for?

2. What is the purpose of a P.O.P.?

3. What materials may be used to produce a promotional display? A permanent kiosk?

4. How does placement of the display affect the P.O.P.'s success?

exercises

1. Visit three different types of stores (for instance, a grocery store, a clothing store- and a fine-gifts store). Keep a log of every point-of-purchase display you see in each store. How are they different? In what ways were the displays successful? How might they have been improved? Save this log with your other package design notes.

2. Choose at least two of the P.O.P. patterns in this chapter and construct them from Bristol or cardboard.

3. Using the 3-D mock-up you designed after Chapter 4, design a P.O.P. display for the package. Begin by sketching ideas for the display and finish by creating a detailed drawing of your idea using either drawing media or the computer. How well does your design display the product? Does it have the same "character" as the packaging?

CHAPTER

"A strong creative portfolio is your number-one career tool. It shows prospective clients or employers who you are and what you can do. It also speaks volumes about your talents and abilities."

The Creative Group

Chapter Objectives

Explore portfolio formats

Assemble a portfolio

Photograph work

Introduction

Learning the techniques necessary to design packages and create mock-ups will not automatically mean the phone will ring with job offers. Clients and other prospective employers in the creative arts, perhaps more than any other field, look for more than a list of acquired skills when hiring. How is it that two designers with the same levels of skill and training can progress so differently—one producing challenging, creative work and moving along the track toward Senior Partner, and the other working primarily outside the design field except for the occasional freelance assignment? Chances are that the

Credit: www.portfolios.com

figure | 8-1 |

More than ever before, a strong digital presentation will lead to greater exposure.

former has mastered the "intangibles" of good portfolio design and presentation, making contacts within the profession and maintaining professional affiliations in graphics and packaging. This chapter will take a look at these areas of self-marketing and promotion.

WHO NEEDS A PORTFOLIO?

figure | 8-2 |

The personal portfolio is a strong self-marketing and promotion tool.

The artist's portfolio is one of the most important tools a designer needs to find jobs and promote his or her work. It offers examples of previous work the designer has produced; displays the designer's level of skill, creativity, and professionalism; adds credibility to a proposal; and serves not only as a foot in the door but also as a conversation starter when seeking new work from a client, an art director, or other employers. In fact, a portfolio is so crucial to landing design jobs and assignments that it's safe to say that there are very few successful designers that could get by without one.

What Is a Portfolio?

A portfolio is a visual record of work. It shows examples of graphic design produced, as either original pieces or re-productions, and gives viewers an indication of the designer's style, talent, past performances, and clients. It should be designed to show the work in the best possible light, often serving as a designer's spokesperson.

All good portfolios share basic elements, but their style, size, format, and presentation all vary.

figure | 8-3 |

There are many different styles of portfolios to choose from; let the work and type of presentation direct the format.

CHOOSING THE PORTFOLIO FORMAT

There are as many different ways to create a portfolio as there are designers.

Style, attitude, media, and audience all play important roles in choosing the appropriate way to showcase graphic design work. There are, however, three basic formats that most portfolios take, and each has specific strengths and weakness to evaluate:

- **The Book Portfolio.** The book portfolio is far and away the most common format used by graphic designers. It consists of a series of pages of flat work, prints, or photographs protected by a durable cover. Often, these pages, sometimes sleeved in acetate or vinyl, are bound by either sewn or spiral binding to hold the pages in place. Covers are typically made of leather, vinyl, or cloth-covered cardboard, though the imagination is the limit and many very effective portfolio covers stray from the norm, with such diverse materials as wood, steel, acrylic, or Plexiglas. In this style of portfolio, the material is meant to be viewed page by page, just as if turning through a book or magazine.

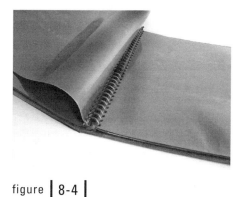

figure | 8-4 |

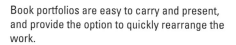

Book portfolios are easy to carry and present, and provide the option to quickly rearrange the work.

Advantages:

- The type of portfolio is easly transported.

- The work is arranged easily.

- The format makes for a very natural presentation.

- The designer has control over the order in which the work is viewed; it's a simple matter of rearranging the pages prior to a presentation to restructure the emphasis of the book, allowing it to be tailor-made to each viewing.

Disadvantages:

- All work displayed in this type of portfolio must be presented as flat images, meaning that 3-D packaging must be photographed or rendered two-dimensionally.

- Work best viewed as a handheld piece looses that interaction when presented flat.

- **The Box Portfolio.** This form of portfolio is very different from the above example. The box portfolio is a box that holds the objects to be presented. The box itself must be of a high quality and project a professional image; work carried to a presentation in a lettuce crate will be perceived as cheap and unprofessional. Individual pieces are sometimes separated by dividers within the box to keep them from sliding, banging into each other, and becoming disordered. Most will also have a lid to cover the pieces and protect them while being transported, and some may even have drop-down front and side panels that lay flat when opened to provide a larger presentation area.

figure | 8-5 |

A box portfolio, like the one above, protects two- or three-dimensional work while maintaining a professional presentation.

Advantages:

- Box portfolios enable the designer to include actual three-dimensional packages or mock-ups in their portfolios.

- Handheld work may be shown in its best light.

Disadvantages:

- These portfolios can be cumbersome and awkward. Transporting them from studio to car to conference room is inconvenient, and the boxes are often scuffed and scraped in the process from bumping against car trunks, elevator doors, or hallway walls, marring the box.

- The designer has no control over the order in which pieces are viewed, in the event he or she is asked to leave the portfolio with a client or art director.

- **The Online Portfolio.** Increasingly, online portfolios are becoming not only a good idea for designers, but a business necessity. Many people looking to hire staff or freelance artists begin with a Web search before they even place an ad or send out word-of-mouth feelers. Obviously, if a designer does not have a presence on the Internet, their name will not come up in these searches. Online portfolios can take many forms. Posting work on a free Web space such as Geocities.com or Yahoo.com is inexpensive and simple, since they usually provide Web page templates for those who don't know how to create pages from scratch. The professional designer may not want to live with the banner and pop-up ads that most often accompany these free sites, though. In that case, another option may be to subscribe to one (or more) of the commercial portfolio hosting sites available. Web sites like Portfolios.com or Coroflot.com rent space to graphic designers and fine artists at varying levels of exposure. Many provide minimal pages (1–5 images) for free, 10–20 images at a paid rate, and "premium" pages (often 20–40 images with "featured status" and more site referrals) at an even higher rate. This is definitely a strength-in-numbers proposition; since so many portfolios can be found at the same Web site with a searchable database, those looking for artists have an easier time viewing work when they visit the featured status sites more regularly. The other choice, of course, is for a designer (or group of designers) to register their own domain name and set up Web pages without ads or pop-ups. The reason the professional might consider this is that, except for the domain registration fees, the artists are free to post as much work as they want without a predetermined ceiling. Also, the designer has complete control over content. One more thing—with this choice, the graphic artist can set up his or her own e-mail account, so that the e-mail address distributed on business cards, flyers, and other promotional material can have a name like *bob@greatdesign.com* as opposed to *bob@artist/graphicdesign/packaging/ freeport folios*, making it easier for clients to find and remember.

Courtesy of portfolios.com

figure | 8-6 |

Increasingly, the online portfolio is becoming a necessary tool in package design service marketing.

Advantages:

- Quick discovery during a Web search.

- Accessibility, and exposure through various Web promotional features.

- Inexpensive distribution to as many people as are reachable.

- Easily and endlessly updateable.

- Perhaps most importantly, demonstrates to potential clients that the designer is computer-literate (or at least knows how to find people who are), which is more and more imperative in the graphics field.

Disadvantages:

- The sense of distance from a package design a viewer experiences when seeing the 3-D object presented on-screen can take a lot away from the encounter.

- Although people without computers and a certain degree of Internet comfort level are becoming harder to find, they do still exist, and a portfolio that exists only in the digital realm will never cross their path.

- **The CD (compact disc) or DVD (digital video disc) Portfolio.** Finally, a growing number of designers have found that burning their portfolios to optical discs such as CDs or DVDs enables them to distribute their work cheaply and easily, either through hand-to-hand distribution or through the mail, directly where the portfolio may have the most impact. All that is needed to produce a CD portfolio is a CD or DVD RW-drive, a computer with digital-imaging software and the know-how to produce consistent, high-quality images of graphic design and packaging work. The key to a good digital portfolio is to choose the images carefully, work only with clear, sharp and compelling photographs, and include information regarding each portfolio piece either in the image itself or as a separate file for easy reference.

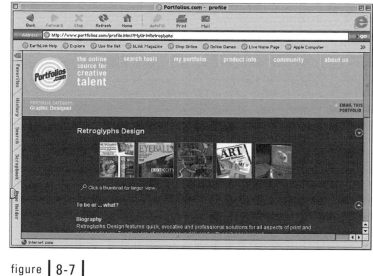

figure | 8-7 |

The online portfolio of Retroglyphs Design on portfolios.com.

| **TIPS** |

Creating an online portfolio enables potential clients to find you on *their* schedule—seven days a week, at any time of day or night. It puts your best work just a few clicks away from those you most want to reach.

figure | 8-8 |

Be certain the CD or DVD portfolio will function on both PC or Macintosh operating systems.

figure | 8-9 |

VINE360, a design group based in Edina, Minnesota, produced this promotional digital and print portfolio for prospective clients. A tin container holds a booklet of the studio's capabilities, a CD of work, and several coasters displaying the studio logo.

Advantages:

- Portfolios on disc are fairly simple to produce and cheap to reproduce; with compact discs now available at under a dollar apiece, it has become less expensive to burn digital images than to make photocopies.

- For a package designer to display his or her computer and digital-imaging prowess is always a plus, since the hardware and software demands upon the professional designer working today continue to grow.

- Each portfolio distributed can be tailor-made to a particular recipient, with work rearranged and re-edited to meet specific needs and goals.

- The designs can be presented in very high resolutions—impossible when dealing with the download times of Internet images.

Disadvantages:

- Like it or not, graphic artists live in a parallel-universe working environment; most designers (and printers and service bureaus) use Apple/Macintosh computer operating systems when producing their work, but a substantial number in the professional world—particularly office managers and human resource staff—prefer computers that are PC(IBM) based. That creates a dilemma for the artist producing a CD portfolio. Should the work be Macintosh compatible for the art director or designer who will be viewing it, or PC compatible for the office staff who may be weeding through applicants? The answer, of course, is both, if at all possible. It won't do any good to create a beautiful presentation for a Mac-based art director if it won't make it through the initial cut by the PC-based screener, and a knock-'em-dead presentation for the human resource crew won't mean anything if the art director can't view it on his or her own computer. Those generating disc portfolios should be sure to find software that will work equally well on either computer platform, or use two separate applications, labeling them on the disc as PC or Mac compatible.

After reading about the different formats a packaging portfolio should take, it may seem confusing as to which direction to go. Book? Box? Online? Disc? If you're looking for any easy answer, the best recommendation by almost every professional portfolio consultant is to design a wide range of portfolios. A designer today needs at least two of the four listed above; three or four would be better. That's because preferences vary among those evaluating the work. Some prefer the hands-on interaction of real, tangible artwork. Others enjoy the convenience of an online presentation that can be called up and viewed at a moment's notice, from home, office, or even on the road. Disc portfolios are easy to share, are much more portable and simple to store than larger books, and can be kept on file long after the main portfolio has gone back to the artist.

One of the more effective presentations is a book portfolio with good, well-composed, high-resolution photographs of three-dimensional pieces, accompanied by one or two actual mock-ups carried on the side. Leaving the client or art director with a disc version of the portfolio—or, at the least, a Web address for online pieces—keeps the portfolio working for the designer after the presentation has ended.

Assembling the Portfolio

Design portfolios should contain between ten and fourteen pieces of the very strongest work the artist has to offer. Many designers make the mistake of trying to include every piece they've produced, but the average viewer will feel overwhelmed and uncomfortable with so many images. More importantly, it's unlikely that all the work will be stellar, which may leave an impression of unevenness and lower the overall impact of the portfolio. Self-editing is the key. If in doubt, the designer should look for advice from a colleague as to whether a particular piece should be inserted or left out. Ten excellent examples will always make for a stronger review than ten that are excellent and five that are so-so.

Regardless of the format, the very best several examples of work should be placed to the front. These are followed by six or so solid designs. The presentation should finish off with another "bang" project—something to leave a strong, favorable impression on the viewer. Why this style of ordering? With most portfolio reviews, the designer and reviewer meet, exchange pleasantries, and delve into the book. The strongest pieces will establish credibility and interest right from the start. As the interview continues, more time is spent talking about ideas, clients, and the designer's experiences, and less time looking at the work. By the end of the presentation, the focus shifts back to the examples.

Assembling a Perfect Package Design Portfolio

Tips from The Creative Group (www.creativegroup.com)

Presenting a portfolio can pose a challenge. Some employers want to see the physical packages you have created, while others prefer viewing only images of your work. If you're meeting with a hiring manager, the best approach is to ask if he or she would like you to bring some of the actual packages you have designed, in addition to your portfolio. If so, you'll want to carry these items separately from your book. A neat box that's "branded" with your contact information and logo is the best type of container for 3-D items. Be cautious about bringing too many of these pieces in addition to your portfolio; less is typically more.

Here are some tips for creating your portfolio:

- **Display only your best work.** Including ten to twelve samples is optimal, but if you have just seven strong pieces, showcase only those items. Advertising and marketing executives surveyed by The Creative Group said they expect an average of eleven pieces to be included in a creative portfolio and typically know whether an individual is qualified after viewing as few as nine items.

- **Showcase your samples with style.** Use a high-quality professional portfolio that allows you to mount individual pieces on a firm mat or backing. If you will be targeting your portfolio to different industries, use a container that allows you to switch out the pieces you display. Keep in mind that, as a package designer, your portfolio is your own personal packaging, so make it neat and distinctive.

- **Present the whole picture.** Photographs of the packages you've designed should be high quality, and you may want to show the piece from different vantage points. Be sure to provide information on the design challenge behind the piece, the name of the client, and the outcome where possible.

- **Show your range.** Consider including strong non packaging pieces you've produced as well. Many hiring managers appreciate versatility and will be impressed by work that demonstrates a strong eye for design.

- **Put your pieces online.** A Web portfolio allows hiring managers to view your samples easily and around the clock. Be sure to organize your work effectively, linking to the various types of packaging you have produced. You'll also want to include a professional biography on your site and contact information on every page.

The Creative Group is a specialized staffing service placing creative, advertising, marketing, and Web professionals with a variety of companies on a project basis. Visit *www.creative-group.com* to learn more about their services and read their online career magazine for creative professionals.

PHOTOGRAPHING 3-D WORK

If three-dimensional packages and mock-ups are to be included in a book or online portfolio, the designs will need to be photographed. Many design studios and packaging consultancies have someone on either staff or retainer trained in and equipped for professional studio photography. These photographers are skilled in creating enticing product shots with photo backdrops, props, and sophisticated lighting. While professional camera work should be chosen for advertising campaigns, P.O.P. displays, and catalog images, perfectly adequate photographs can be produced using simple equipment and a little creativity for use on the Web or in a portfolio.

Equipment

The first thing required for photography, of course, is a camera. In the past, a good 35-mm camera would have been a must, but today many digital cameras are available that are affordable and of sufficient quality to provide excellent results. Another plus of using a digital camera: the steps of photo processing and scanning are eliminated, saving time and money. Images can be imported directly into photo-enhancing software, where they are easily cropped, adjusted, and printed. It is essential, however, that whatever camera is used, it has either a cable shutter release or a self-timer option to take shake-free pictures.

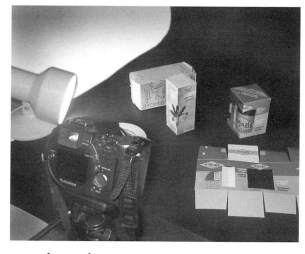

figure | 8-10 |

Photographing three-dimensional work is sometimes the best way to display it in a portfolio.

In addition to the camera, though, there are several other pieces of equipment required:

- **Tripod.** It will be almost impossible to make do without a tripod to steady the camera, compose the photograph, and properly focus the image.

- **Lights.** Every photo should be properly lit. If using natural lighting, an overcast day will often provide excellent diffused light without harsh shadows. Translucent light-diffusers can also be used if the sunlight is too bright. If shooting inside with artificial lighting, it's probably wise to invest in some balanced lights to avoid unnatural color shifts, which are common with fluorescent and normal incandescent lights. At least two lights are recommended—one to fall on the subject and another to bounce off a screen reflector or ceiling to soften the shadows.

figure | 8-11 |

Setup for photographing portfolio piece.

- **Photo stage.** A photo stage or copy stage is a table or other raised platform that allows the package to be photographed at or near eye level. It will bring the entire subject up where it can be arranged comfortably. An ordinary table will work fine for this purpose.

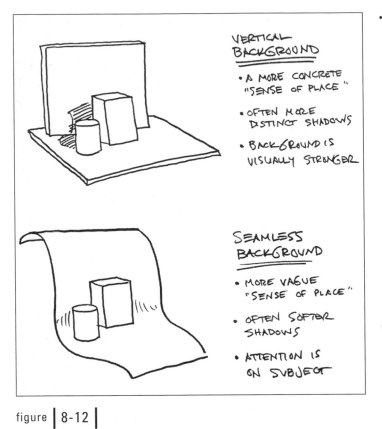

VERTICAL
BACKGROUND

- A MORE CONCRETE "SENSE OF PLACE"
- OFTEN MORE DISTINCT SHADOWS
- BACKGROUND IS VISUALLY STRONGER

SEAMLESS
BACKGROUND

- MORE VAGUE "SENSE OF PLACE"
- OFTEN SOFTER SHADOWS
- ATTENTION IS ON SUBJECT

figure | 8-12 |

The two basic types of backdrops: the vertical backdrop and a seamless background.

- **Backdrops.** Backdrops make it possible for the photographer to change the environment in which the package will appear. For basic object photography, either a "seamless" backdrop or a "perpendicular" backdrop may be used (see Figure 8-12). Generally, a seamless backdrop will create softer object shadows and focus the viewer's attention on the package itself. A perpendicular backdrop will create sharper shadows and "place" the package more than the seamless. It's normally advised to avoid busy backdrops, as these will distract and draw attention away from the subject. Instead, white, black, or neutral backdrops are preferred.

- **Props.** Sometimes it's desireable to depict the package in a setting. In this case, props—other objects placed around the package—can help to add a feeling of context to the photograph. Props can be as simple as a coffee cup or a set of car keys, or as complex as a fully re-created scene.

Design by Jessica Baechle

figure | 8-13 |

A packaging mock-up shot against a black seamless background. The incorporation of props—in this case, flowers and rose petals—enhance the photograph for use in an ad.

Setting up the Shot

When composing the picture, the package is placed on the photo stage with the desired backdrop, and the camera is positioned at the appropriate angle. Sometimes, this means shooting from directly above the subject. More often, the camera is aligned at eye level with the package. The most effective angle can be found by experimenting with the camera position. Shooting from too high or too low a vantage point will result in "key stoning" of the package, exaggerating the perspective and causing it to appear either very small or towering. Key stoning will also distort type and graphics of the package design, and should only occur when that is the desired effect.

Props can be placed around the package or it can be photographed against the empty backdrop. Again, trying many different arrangements can lead to more interesting photographs. If using props, care should be taken that they do not obscure important information on the package; they should reinforce the package and not overpower it.

Proper lighting placement is crucial to achieve the right portrayal of the scene. Bright lights should not shine directly onto a label as they will wash out typography, logos, or surface graphics in the photo. Instead, indirect light or light bounced off a reflector screen (this can be as simple as a clean sheet of white mat board or foam core) or ceiling will illuminate the subject more evenly.

Once the composition, angle, and lighting are right, the photo can be made. If the camera has automatic focusing, the photographer must make certain that the package (or other portion of the scene that must be in focus and crisp) falls within the focus frame of the camera. If manual focus is used, the focus ring on the camera lens is turned until the desired area of the scene is in sharp focus.

Using either a self-timer on the camera or a cable release will minimize any camera movement during the exposure and will provide a more clear image.

While the composition is set up, it's always worthwhile to make several exposures. Change the aperture of the camera or the intensity of light. This is called bracketing the exposure, and better ensures that at least one of the shots will be suitable, saving time later. Remember, also, that many brightness and contrast issues can be adjusted within photo-imaging software such as Adobe Photoshop, but an out-of-focus or blurry photo cannot be corrected.

DESIGNING GREEN:
RESPONSIBILTY IN PACKAGING

For a growing number of consumers, the environmental impact of packaging has a powerful influence on product acceptance. As a result, industries and designers alike are looking for more alternatives in packaging material choices and greater efficiency in their uses. This means that the traditional timeline of a package—its travel from forest, to paper mill, to store shelf, to landfill—is evolving into one of greater renewability and accountability.

Design by Jessica Baechle

figure | 8-14 |

Design by Jason Koebel

figure | 8-15 |

Adding a few simple props to this setup puts the product actively into the imagination and life of the viewer.

Products such as breakfast cereals have long relied on a large "shelf face" to shoulder out competing brands, meaning that packaging is typically 30 percent to 40 percent larger than required to hold the contents. In 2001, the EPA estimates that almost 82 million tons of paper and paperboard waste were generated in the U.S. Of that, almost 37 million tons—or 45 percent—were recycled, and the percentages rise each year. Today's graphic designer can, and should, consider packaging options while producing creative work. The variety of papers and cardboards with recycled content is constantly growing, making it easy for designers to choose boards with a 10 to 30 percent recycled content when specifying box materials for production. When a package must be produced from virgin tree fiber, the materials are certified by the Forest Stewardship Council (FSC) and come from environmentally responsible forest management and restoration practices.

Recyclable plastics, aluminum, glass, and cardboards—especially those free of leads, halogens, mercury, PVC/HPEC, Styrofoam, or other noxious or hazardous materials—are both environment- and consumer-friendly. Legislators, pressure groups, and concerned consumers are bringing the issues of "green" packaging to the forefront of economic and political agendas. Today's designer must meet the challenge by creating attractive, protective packaging that answers not only the issue of recycling and resources, but also aesthetics.

Steps to More Responsible Package Design

How can a designer work to create more "green" packaging?

- **Eliminate unnecessary packaging.** Excessive packaging is both wasteful and expensive. Designers should weigh the impact of the design with environmental concerns. Trends are already under way with up-scale and Earth-friendly companies (particularly in natural food and cosmetics areas) toward minimal package material, where it does not compromise protection of the contents.

- **Specify environmentally safe materials.** Packaging materials that are recyclable or biodegradable not only reduce the waste stream, they are increasingly preferred by shoppers. In fact, many consumers base their buying decisions on environmental concerns.

- **Consider designing "reusable" packaging.** Packages that may be refilled or otherwise reused serve a number of functions. First, they are more desirable to consumers because of convenience and the implication of a greater intrinsic value. Second, they have a longer "keep life," meaning they are more likely to stay in consumer view for a much longer time (which is exposure for the design and brand) and to encourage repeat sales of refills.

SUMMING IT UP

The portfolio is the clearest demonstration a graphic artist has of the work he or she can produce, and the best indication a client has for what they can expect. Every care possible should be taken that the portfolio is clean, accurate, and presented with professionalism. By creating portfolios in varying formats, the designer has a better chance of effectively marketing his or her work.

It's also worth noting that, in a very real sense, the portfolio should be a constantly evolving thing; the most productive presentations are tailor-made to fit precise situations. No portfolio can, or should, be considered a one-size-fits-all solution to every scenario. Is this a portfolio for acceptance into a school? Is it made of student work to land that first job? Should it display a broad range of skills or be specifically targeted to appeal to one particular market? These are all questions that should be asked while preparing for the presentation, and answered by the work included in the portfolio, the ordering of pieces, and the format it will take.

As new work is created, the portfolio will transform. Pieces will be added, others removed. And that's how it should be, because a changing, developing portfolio is a reflection of an ever-stronger design sense and artistic growth.

review questions

1. Why do package designers need portfolios? What functions do they serve?

2. What are the four formats of portfolios discussed in this chapter?

3. The usual design portfolio consists of how many work examples?

4. What are some typical ways to enhance photographs of packaging work?

exercises

1. Visit a store that specializes in artist portfolios. View firsthand the various options and make notes on potential advantages and disadvantages of each.

2. After photographing some of your work, create a simple online portfolio. You may use any Web page development software you are familiar with, or the Web Photo Gallery function in Adobe Photoshop.

3. Practice showing your portfolio to a colleague or friend. How does the presentation flow? Rehearse it several times until you are comfortable displaying and discussing your work.

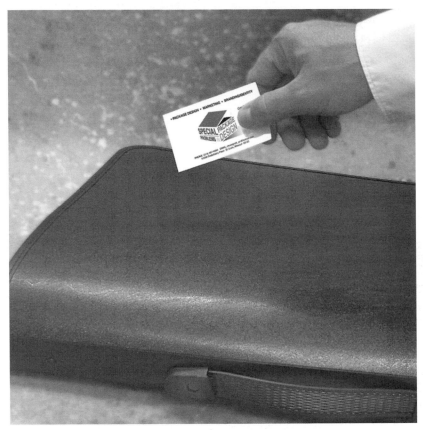

CHAPTER

"Work your tail off and try to pursue everything you are interested in, even if it may seem, for now, not to have that much to do with packaging design. Associate yourself with people whose work you admire and give it everything you've got. Be open to the kind of painful criticism and self-evaluation that is a necessary part of an endeavor like this, but at the same time, stick to your convictions. Be willing to risk failure. And don't forget to have fun."

—Randy Mosher, owner, Randy Mosher Design

Chapter Objectives

Review concepts

Apply what you've learned

Take a glance at professional affiliations and organizations

Introduction

After reading about the history of packaging, the techniques and tools, Gestalt psychology, and producing a portfolio, do you have a different feeling when walking down the supermarket aisle? Do you hear the packages speaking to you (sometimes even shouting) from the shelves?

figure | 9-1 |

Do you hear the packages shouting from the shelves?

figure | 9-2 |

New software is impacting the field of package design.
Tridimage / 3D Packaging Image Design (www.tridimage.com)

Packaging is one of the more challenging disciplines within graphic design, but it's also among the least represented, in terms of college curricula and number of designers in the field. As the public becomes more and more savvy to the effect of package design on their buying habits and lifestyles, the designers' understanding of reaching their audience must keep pace.

This is an exciting time in package design. Emerging software, evolving use of materials, an enhanced appreciation for "green" packaging and the environment—we are on a threshold where designers have greater freedom of packaging form, media, and message. For the designer ready and compelled to take the leap to 3-D design, the opportunities are there.

HISTORY REPEATS ITSELF

When we look at the influences around us, it's remarkable how cyclical our culture is. That paisley shirt from the '70s—don't throw it away!—it's back in style. Your dad listened to Led Zeppelin (you swore you never would) and today your kids are playing air guitar to "Stairway to Heaven."

figure | 9-3 |

Psychedelic poster art from the 1960s—heavily influenced by
1890s graphics—is making a comeback.

It's no wonder that designers, attuned to the visual flavor of the month, understand that, to be ahead of the curve for the future, it's important to have a grasp of the past. What's come before has a direct link to how we express ourselves today. Look at typography: Art Nouveau type of the 1890s came back into vogue in the psychedelic poster art of the 1960s—and has currently returned again in all areas of the graphic arts. Fashions move the same way, as do color palettes and compositional concerns.

Any designer working today should have a firm grasp of the history of package design. Robert Gair, Alexander Parkes, Louis Cheskin—each has made a significant contribution to the craft, and designers today cannot move forward without a knowledge of the history of the field.

BOARD SKILLS

Good board skills are essential for the communicative designer. In this book, you have learned about the various skills and techniques necessary for package design and the production of professional mock-ups. Most of these skills focused on the traditional methods of hand-to-board design, because these are the foundations for craftsmanship and graphic communication. The aim was to present a broad but thorough look at the tools—and their use—commonly found in professional design studios. Another reason these traditional skills are emphasized is that most computer software used in package design almost invariably takes its cue directly from these techniques. The designer with a grasp of the *concept* of what he or she is attempting to accomplish can easily adapt and transition from one software to another to achieve the desired goal.

figure | 9-4 |

Practice makes difficult tasks easier. Print a series of circles and curves to perfect X-Acto cutting technique.

By following the descriptions and illustrations and completing the exercises in each chapter, these skills were introduced and reinforced. Don't worry if they do not come easily at first; for those who are persistent, they will come. And once mastered, they will open up an entirely new world of visual expression for the designer, moving communication from the flat, 2-D realm into rich, accurate, design-in-the-round.

It comes down to the ever-stated advice: practice, practice, practice. Have trouble cutting curves with an X-Acto knife? Then, cut curves all day. It's like a baseball player in a batting cage. Learn the correct method and repeat it over and over until it's ingrained. Soon, it all becomes second nature.

EXPERIMENTING WITH FORM

Chapter 6 of this book was devoted entirely to presenting more than fifty accurate 2-D patterns to follow to create some standard and some not-so-standard 3-D package forms. Care was taken to represent all four of the basic shapes: the cube, pyramid, cone, and cylinder, as well as several more inventive shapes that extend beyond the envelope to show just a fraction of the possibilities of paperboard packaging. To emphasize: the patterns here are just starting points. The inquisitive designer will learn these forms and leap off into countless directions. Because once these fundamentals are learned, the forms open themselves up into unending variations. Alter a single dimension and the character of the whole package changes.

figure 9-5 |

Cornhusk packaging provides this Central American sugar with a natural and traditional feel.

PROFILES

Tadashi Isozaki

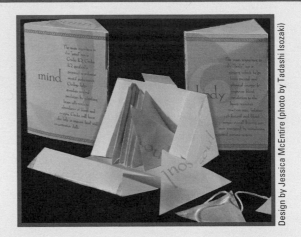

Design by Jessica McEntire (photo by Tadashi Isozaki)

You'll often find Tadashi Isozaki in his office after hours, preparing student assignments and lectures or evaluating finished work. Isozaki teaches package design at the University of Kansas in Lawrence, Kansas—a university with almost 30,000 students—1,200 of whom are in the Art and Design programs. Class sizes vary, but Isozaki says most of the packaging classes average between twelve and twenty students. "I don't only teach packaging," he says, "I teach students graphic design principles and how to develop their conceptual approach through 2D, 3D, and interactive design . . . all the work they do will be part of their portfolio which will help them land somewhere."

His own education had Isozaki studying graphic design at Fort Hays (Kansas) State University, where mentor Chaiwat Thumsujarit introduced him to package design. "Professor Thumsujarit guided me to focus on the importance of a conceptual approach. There were problem-solving projects, such as making a paper clock with only paper but no adhesives, or taking six ordinary buttons and thinking of a new and attractive way to package them, that challenged me to study the problem and

figure | 9-6 |

Experimenting with nonstandard packaging materials and structures can yield surprising results.

The most vital aspect of package design is function. The function of containment, the function of protection, the function of display—in essence, the function of taking a design and giving it physicality. Too often, designers become enamored with a package's shape and structure and try to force a design to fit it, when the opposite should be true. Always let the concept guide the design, instead of the other way around.

Experiment with these patterns. See what they yield. Don't limit yourself to set formulae, but take each design as a challenge and an opportunity to expand your own experiences.

Package design is a cumulative art. Each step of the process builds upon the last. Brainstorming leads to sketches, which approach it from different angles." Isozaki also looks to the graphic design work of Japan for inspiration. "There are so many creative packaging designs in Japan. Some of these concepts include a traditional appreciation of nature and an emphasis on using design to generate emotional responses. Nature has been a dominant theme of Japanese design, and it appears in Japanese packaging for traditional products. Graphic designers have captured this old spirit of Japan by using wonderful colors, patterns, Kanji (Chinese character) calligraphy, and by choosing materials for specific purposes in a very conscious way."

"As I mentioned, I started looking back at my own origin, Japanese culture, since I started teaching at KU. I think it's important to familiarize designers with both traditional and contemporary conceptual and technological practices that they will encounter in their professional careers. In addition, it is important that designers in the 21st century be exposed to global perspectives, and one way to achieve this is by emphasizing international design."

When evaluating a packaging solution, either as a consumer or as an instructor, Isozaki considers first the idea. "Design must be creative, reasonable, and functional," he says. "I look for the creative concept behind a product, by looking at the paper folding technique, shape, label shape, textures, colors, and size in order to make the product more attractive to both designers and consumers than the others on the shelf.

"I believe the underlining principle is to apply the design concept and execute it in balance. It is a matter of how designers apply the concept, whether working two-dimensionally or three-dimensionally. There must be creative concept in any medium of designing. It is essential to see the value of thinking 'outside the box' while respecting the fundamentals of design. I believe this approach will flow over into any artistic project, as well as impress potential viewers." ■

lead to concepts, then to engineering structure, creating a mock-up, and on and on until the work appears on a shop shelf. But, in a broader sense, each solution created becomes a stepping-stone along the path of a designer's development as an artist and a communicator.

SHOWING THE WORK

After the study, the training, and the mastering of skills, the time comes to show the work. For most, this means putting together a professional portfolio and developing a presentation to be viewed by product clients, art directors, and hiring managers. This stage of the game requires every bit as much attention, effort, and

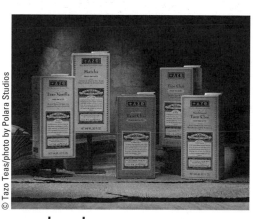

© Tazo Teas/photo by Polara Studios

figure | 9-7 |

Tazo has helped define the upscale tea experience.

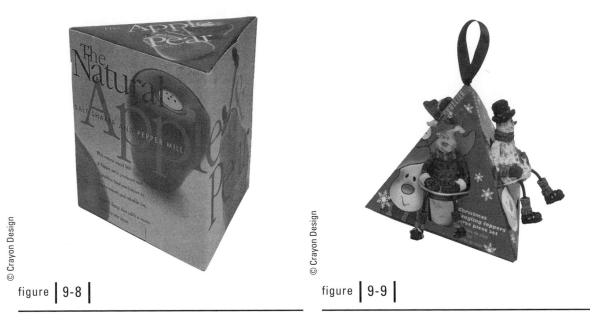

© Crayon Design

figure | 9-8 |

This triangular package sets it apart from others on the shelf.

© Crayon Design

figure | 9-9 |

Packaged as a tree ornament, these holiday bottle toppers break the boundries of their pyramid container.

preparation as producing the work itself. The portfolio presentation is usually the only chance a designer has to meet with prospective clients and not only impress them with the creativity and professionalism of past work, but also convey an attitude, inquisitiveness, confidence, and personality the client will feel comfortable working with and trusting with their product's appearance. Craftsmanship of the portfolio must be impeccable. In addition, it's a good idea to practice the verbal description of the pieces. Find a friend or colleague to rehearse with. In this way, you can learn to describe your work with self-assurance and learn to field unexpected questions. These rehearsals will also give some valuable feedback as to the pace and flow of the presentation and the consistency of the work, as well as help you to feel more at ease in talking about your designs.

There are many career consultants, informative books, and Web sites aimed at helping you hone your job search and interview skills. Take advantage of them. They will provide résumé and cover-letter-writing tips, interviewing advice, networking opportunities, and salary negotiation insights.

| TIPS |

A portfolio presentation has a lot to do with the impressions you make. Hiring managers at all levels, from large corporations to small, three-member studios, agree it's important to dress appropriately, arrive on time (or even a little early), and be prepared. Know something about the company, client, or product and ask pertinent questions. This shows you know why you're there.

ABOUT PROFESSIONAL AFFILIATIONS AND ORGANIZATIONS

Before you can show your portfolio or interview for a potential job or project, you have to be aware of the opening. This information comes in several ways; to effectively market your work, you should be familiar with all the avenues of learning about these opportunities.

Many designers spend a lot of time poring over the Sunday classified section of the newspaper, looking for "Graphic Artist Wanted" listings. Although this resource should not be ignored—I've personally found several great projects through want ads—it's not where most jobs will come from. For one reason, if you saw the ad, then you can rest assured that thousands of other people did as well. If just 10 percent of those interested in the listing actually answer the ad, you are still facing hundreds of competitive applicants. That means that your résumé or portfolio will be just one of many in the pile; even if you are perfect for the position, it's likely that someone else will be more experienced than you or willing to do the work cheaper.

Far more productive leads will come from referrals or word-of-mouth information. Maintaining active contacts in the graphic design community—locally, nationally, and internationally—will help keep your name in the minds of art directors and clients *before* the job finds its way to the newspaper ad. Many professional design organizations such as AIGA (the American Institute of Graphic Arts), the Graphic Artist Guild, and ICOGRADA (International Council of Graphic Design Associations) have local chapters throughout the country where practicing professionals and students of graphic art meet, discuss the profession, exhibit work, and network. The AIGA alone has over fifty chapters in the United States, and ICOGRADA more than eighty affiliations worldwide. In addition to valuable leads of staff and freelance opportunities, these organizations allow designers to gather, exchange ideas, discuss practical and ethical concerns of the field, promote education and, in some cases, provide legal representation or mediation in design disputes. The Graphic Artists Guild serves as an advocacy group for those working in design and illustration, with resources that range from pricing guidelines and professional development, to information services and health insurance.

At the back of this book, you will find a list of several of the more well-known graphic design organizations, along with their addresses and Web page URLs. Every designer working in the field today should look into the various groups that operate in their area, and determine what they have to offer. Information, resources, and support are valuable commodities

figure | 9-10 |

The American Institute of Graphic Arts, in New York, New York.

figure | 9-11 |

The Graphic Artists Guild publishes the Pricing and Ethical Guidelines as a resource for professionals in the field.

| SURVEY |

Some designers like to know what is happening elsewhere in their field, others don't. How about you?

Are you interested in knowing about the state of graphic design in other countries?

Very interested	**61%**
Just curious	**37%**
Not interested at all	**4%**

Totals shown may be more or less than 100% due to rounding.

SOURCE: The International Council of Graphic Design Associations

to the visual communicator, and the sense of community and shared ideas by designers at all levels of their careers helps to bring a cohesion and unity to the profession as we work to further define the role of design in both business and society.

SUMMING IT UP

Packaging, one of the more challenging of areas in graphic design, requires a broad view of the field. An awareness of the history of packaging, knowledge of materials and structures, an understanding of portfolio assembly and presentation, and professional affiliations are all necessary for a successful entrance into the arena of packaging and 3-D design. This book has attempted to acquaint the reader with just such a view. Chapter by chapter—and reinforced by the color section of exceptional packaging work from around the world—the practical aspects of 3-D package design have been presented. Through the principles and techniques outlined here, the reader will gain a better awareness and more comprehensive appreciation of the field of package design.

Further Reading

- BENNETT, JAMES GORDON. *Design Fundamentals for New Media* (Thomson/Delmar Learning, 2005)

- CLIFF, STAFFORD. *50 Trade Secrets of Great Design: Packaging* (Rockport Publishers, Inc., 2001)

- HINE, THOMAS. *The Total Package* (Little, Brown and Company, 1997)

- JANKOWSKI, JERRY. *Shelf Life* (Chronicle Books, 1992)

- JENNINGS, SIMON. *Advanced Illustrations and Design* (Chartwell Books, Inc., 1987)

- ROBINSON, WAYNE. *How'd They Design and Print That?* (North Light Books, 1991)

- ROTH, LASZLO / WYBENGA, GEORGE L. *The Packaging Designer's Book of Patterns* (John Wiley & Sons, Inc., 2000)

- SPIEKERMANN, ERIK / GINGER, E.M. *Stop Stealing Sheep* & *Find Out How Type Works* (Adobe Press, 1993)

Professional Graphic Design and Packaging Organizations

- American Institute of Graphic Arts (www.aiga.org)

- Association of Graphic Communications (www.agcomm.org)

- Association of Professional Design Firms (www.apdf.org)

- Corporate Design Foundation (www.cdf.org)

- Flexible Packaging Association (www.fpa.org)

- Graphic Artists Guild (www.gag.org)

- International Council of Graphic Design Associations (www.icograda.org)

- Institute of Packaging Professionals (www.iopp.org)

- Japan Package Design Association (www.jpda.cr.jp)

- Paperboard Packaging Council (www.ppcnet.org)

- Society of Typographic Aficionados—S(o)FA (www.typesociety.org)

- Union Latino Americana del Embalage—ULADE (www.packaging.com.ar)

- Women in Packaging (www.womeninpackaging.org)

- World Packaging Organisation (www.packaging-technology.com/wpo)

Portfolio Resources and Web Sites
Free and Commercial Portfolio Web sites

- Coroflot (www.coroflot.com)

- Portfolios.com (www.portfolios.com)

- Qfolio—Online Portfolio Service for Artists and Designers (www.qfolio.com)

- The Creative Group—Creating a Winning Portfolio (www.creativegroup.com/TCG/winningportfolio)

index

INDEX